Alms for Oblivion

Peter Kemp

v. 1

First paperback edition by Mystery Grove Publishing Co. LLC

NOTE FROM THE PUBLISHER

First published in 1961, *Alms for Oblivion* is the final book in Peter Kemp's trilogy of memoirs that took readers through the most destructive period in recorded history. His first book, *Mine Were of Trouble*, chronicled his adventures while volunteering for the Nationalists during the Spanish Civil War. Its darker sequel, *No Colours or Crest*, followed Kemp through the Second World War as a commando and later guerilla liaison in Eastern Europe. Picking up almost immediately after the disastrous events of that book, *Alms for Oblivion* sees Kemp in the South Pacific at the end and aftermath of World War Two.

When readers first met Kemp, he was a young idealist who went forth into the unknown and emerged victorious. Later, fighting for his homeland, he learned that victory is sometimes a bitter pill to swallow. *Alms for Oblivion* sees Kemp in a much comfortable setting than *No Colours or Crest*, but still affected by his experiences. The kindness, bravery, and tenacity of Peter Kemp the volunteer is still there, but Kemp the elder is experienced, jaded, and at times absolutely ruthless. It's his briefest and most personal work.

The book is an unflinching account of the chaotic final days of World War Two. Readers will see Kemp juggle the roles of soldier, smuggler, diplomat, and police officer to bring order to the chaos. Despite offering a unique view of largely unknown but critical events in world history, *Alms for Oblivion* was out-of-print for decades, with the few remaining copies too expensive for the average reader. Mystery Grove Publishing Company is happy and proud to finally make this classic available for the first time in paperback form, allowing Kemp's work to be enjoyed by a new generation.

Please note, although we've attempted to recreate Kemp's work, several photographs appeared in the first edition hardback that would have been too costly to reproduce while keeping prices low. These photos are available free of charge online. Simply contact our Twitter account (@MysteryGrove).

Thank you for reading! It has been a pleasure bringing the books of Peter Kemp, an unsung patriot and hero, back to general circulation. We hope you have enjoyed them and come away with new appreciation of the giants who gave so much for the people and nations they loved so dearly.

Special acknowledgement goes to the men of the HWGC, CL, and Grove Street. Without their support and friendship these releases would not be possible.

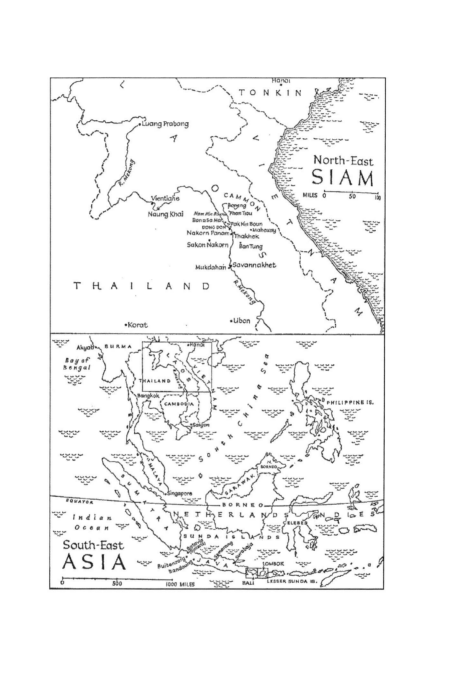

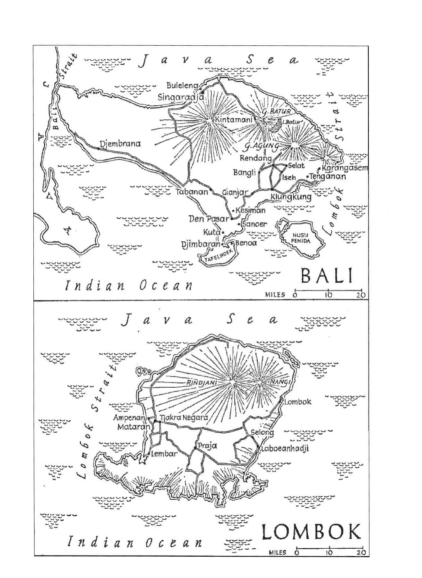

ACKNOWLEDGEMENTS

My particular thanks are due to the following friends:

Colonel David Smiley, M.V.O., O.B.E., M.C., for access to his valuable diaries covering the period August to November 1945; Major the Lord St. Oswald, M.C., for his useful advice and for permission to quote from his signals; General Sir Robert Mansergh, G.C.B., K.B.E., M.C., and General Sir Geoffrey Evans, C.I.E., for details of military operations in which I had the honour to serve under them; Major Daan Hubrecht, Royal Netherlands East Indies Army, for putting at my disposal his unique knowledge of the island of Bali; Lt.-Col. John Shaw, M.C., Royal Horse Guards, for his help in the preparation of the chapters on Bali and Lombok, where we served together; and to Mrs. John Etty-Leal and Mrs. Elizabeth Moore for their indispensable advice and collaboration in the preparation of my typescript.

The quotation from 'Mad Dogs and Englishmen' by Noel Coward is printed by permission of Chappell & Co. Ltd.; the extract from *Island of Bali* by Miguel Covarrubias is printed by permission of Cassell & Co. Ltd.

PETER KEMP

Time hath, my lord, a wallet at his back,
Wherein he puts alms for oblivion

Troilus and Cressida
Act III, Scene 3

TO THE MEMORY
OF MY FRIEND
COLLIN BROOKS

*We shall all meet again in the great
tavern that lies at the end of the world*
G.K. Chesterton

TABLE OF CONTENTS

PROLOGUE

GO EAST, YOUNG MAN

'Well now,' grinned the fat man as he finished his third pint of bitter, 'after your five years' holiday I hope you'll be thinking of settling down to a decent job of work.'

Like many others in uniform I was getting used to this old joke; I made a polite but unconvincing effort to smile. Something, I realized on this May morning in 1945, was gravely wrong with my sense of humour. Outside the stuffy, overcrowded bar with its wrought glass mirrors, enamelled pump handles and remnants of Victorian bric-a-brac, London sparkled in the midday sunlight. The fireworks of V.E. day were barely cold. But already the wine of victory had turned to vinegar; disenchantment had set in. Europe was a desert of rubble whose embittered, starved and disease-ridden population watched with apathy the preparations for a hideous peace. While Russian soldiers raped and murdered in Vienna, Prague and Budapest, Englishmen talked with admiration and affection of good old Uncle Joe, and on V.E. night I had heard voices in the crowd before Buckingham Palace call out, 'Joe for King!'

In truth my own 'holiday' had lasted a good deal longer than five years, for I had first gone to war soon after leaving Cambridge in 1936; I had spent the greater part of the next three years in Spain, serving in the Nationalist armies—at first in the Carlist Militia and later in the Spanish Foreign Legion. I had joined the Nationalists to fight against Communism, which I believed—and still believe—would have engulfed Spain if the Republicans had won the Civil War. However, in Britain General Franco had not enjoyed a good Press and in the eyes of some of my intellectual friends, for whom an uncritical enthusiasm for everything Russian was, since 1941, the indispensable equipment of a patriot, I was little better than a Fascist; I found it useless to point out that nearly all my companions in Spain had been either monarchists, whose loathing of all totalitarian systems was as strong as my own, or professional soldiers who viewed all politics with suspicion and contempt.

By the end of the Civil War I had seen enough fighting to last me a lifetime and, after severe injuries to my jaw and hands from an enemy mortar bomb, I was temporarily unfit for any more. For the first four months of the European war, therefore, I had been a civilian. But as a result of a chance meeting with a friend in the War Office, followed by an interview in one of the dustier and more depressing rooms of that cheerless building, I soon found myself commissioned into the British Army, in the service of a paramilitary organization that has since became famous under the title of S.O.E. or Special Operations Executive. This organization, whose purpose was to promote subversion in enemy and enemy-occupied territories, has in recent years aroused considerable controversy, attracting from different quarters some excessive praise and much unmerited abuse. For me it proved a first-class travel agency, sending me at His Majesty's expense to countries that I could never otherwise have hoped to visit.

Thus, after taking part in a number of small raids on the coast of France, I had dropped by parachute in the late summer of 1943 into southern Albania; I had travelled on foot and horseback the length of that country until, some nine months later, I was flown from Montenegro to S.O.E. headquarters in southern Italy. Arriving back in England with frayed nerves, corns on my feet and a useful experience of political intrigue, I had dropped in December 1944 into south-western Poland, a member of a small mission to the Polish Underground Army—or what was left of it after the heroism and tragedy of Warsaw. For a month we had eluded German pursuit, owing our lives to the courage and self-sacrifice of our Polish friends: then we had witnessed the sickening spectacle of the Red Army's progress through Poland and its subjection of that incomparable nation. There had followed a month in an N.K.V.D. prison and another month in Moscow before I had returned by slow stages to England, the end of the European war, and the welcome of my fat friend in the pub.

I was worried and ill-tempered as I walked down Piccadilly on my way to lunch with a brother officer. It was all very well, I reflected sourly, to talk about settling down to a decent job of work; but the work we had started in 1939 was not yet done. Large areas of south-east Asia and the Far East were in the hands of an enemy less efficient, perhaps, than the Germans, but still formidable. In any case I was not yet due for demobilization. There was nothing to keep me in England. My marriage had collapsed; I was in the process of a divorce. My private life was an ugly mess. There were plenty of married men in our Far Eastern forces who had not seen their families for years; what conceivable justification could I have for staying at home? I had, too, a more positive reason for going.

On my way home from Russia I had spent several days in Cairo, where I had renewed an old friendship. Major David Smiley, a regular officer in the Household Cavalry, with whom I had worked closely during my first months in Albania, was passing through on his way to the Far East. A year younger than myself, short and wiry, with very bright blue eyes, an alert, inquisitive manner and a jerky, often abrupt style of speech, he concealed behind a disarming modesty and shyness a shrewd, objective mind, a cool judgment and the stoutest heart I have ever known.

Over a delicious lunch of shishkebab and Turkish coffee in a small Arab restaurant he had told me that he was bound for Siam to train and lead guerrillas in operations against the Japanese lines of communication between Indo-China and Malaya; if I cared to join him, all I need do when I reached London was to send him a signal from our office in Baker Street.

Although born in India I knew nothing of the Far East, and had previously felt no urge to go there; but Siam appealed to me as a romantic and little known country, and the prospect of such important and interesting work with Smiley attracted me still more. By the time I reached the club where I was lunching I had made up my mind to go.

The two lieutenant-colonels in the Far Eastern Section of our office in Baker Street were cordial and co-operative.

'We'll signal Smiley right away,' they promised. 'But in any case you needn't worry. There'll be plenty of man's work in Burma and Malaya as well as Siam. Give us a couple of weeks to arrange your transfer to this Section and fix you up with an air passage to India; but you needn't be in too much of a hurry because the monsoon is well under way out there and nothing much is likely to happen in the field just yet. Why don't you take a bit more leave? You could probably do with it after Poland and that Russian prison. Meanwhile, here's Juliet, who's just back from our headquarters in Calcutta— she can probably give you a few useful tips.'

Juliet was a trim and self-possessed young woman with soft brown hair, faultless curves and inviting dark blue eyes. Most of her advice on the Far East proved inaccurate; she did, however, give me a few tips of more lasting value, and she was a sparkling, even bewitching companion and partner in pleasure.

From this exhausting diversion I soon felt obliged to take a short rest; and so I invited myself to stay with some cousins near Dublin. Whether that was the best way to restore my health will be doubted by anyone who remembers the generous hospitality of the southern Irish to members of His Majesty's armed forces on leave in their country. It needed more than a vigorous walk in the Wicklow Hills to work off a heavy drinking session in Davy Byrnne's or the Royal Hibernian; on the other hand there was no breath of disenchantment in the wind that kissed the bracken on the Sugar Loaf, no gleam of cynicism in the sunlight that gilded the stones of Trinity, no suspicion of reserve in the welcome extended me by everyone I met, from the great John McCormack, his vitality undimmed by age and illness, to the porters in the Shelbourne or the peasants in the country around Bray. Most of them, I remembered, had close friends or relatives in the fighting services of the British Commonwealth.

Back in London I stayed in St. John's Wood with Collin Brooks, at that time the Editor of *Truth*; he and his family were old friends of infinite kindness, patience and stamina who had often given me shelter during and before the war. From their house I made daily visits to Baker Street. Juliet was busy giving instruction to another officer; but the two lieutenant-colonels greeted me as cordially as before.

'We've had a signal back from Smiley,' they told me. 'He's dropped into Siam and wants you to join him. You'll have to report first to our base at Kandy; they'll send you on to Calcutta, where you'll find the Siamese Country Section. We've applied for your air passage and we'll let you know as soon as it comes through. Meanwhile, here's Geraldine who's just back from Kandy—she'll probably give you some useful tips.'

Geraldine also had a trim figure. . . . The remainder of my time in London was a frenzied round of parties, bars and night-clubs, which did nothing to restore a constitution already weakened by the two extremes of Russian and Irish hospitality. One morning, fearing that I was sickening for something, I decided to consult a doctor whom I had known for some years. After examining me and asking a number of questions he reached for his prescription pad, scribbled a few words and pushed the piece of paper across the desk.

'I think this should fix you,' he observed drily.

It read simply: 'Say no thank you three times daily.'

Young man, I told myself severely, Go East. A week later I was in India.

I

'EVEN CARIBUS LIE AROUND AND SNOOZE'

My destination was Ceylon: to be exact Kandy, where S.O.E., under its Far Eastern disguise of Force 136, maintained its own headquarters staff among the many that contributed to the glory, and variety, of South-East Asia Command. But my aeroplane would take me no farther than Karachi, where I was consigned to a transit camp on the edge of the Sind Desert, along with a large number of other officers who were southward bound.

Before leaving London I had been well endowed with that sacred gift, Priority, and so it is unlikely that I should have lingered in Karachi had I not, with my faultless genius for putting spokes in my own wheel, developed an acute and laming attack of gout. In the cool and beautifully run R.A.F. hospital I soon recovered; I also learned some disturbing things about the habits of this new enemy I was going to meet.

Among the patients with whom I became friendly was a young subaltern of an Indian infantry regiment, who had been wounded and taken prisoner by the retreating Japanese in Burma; they had tied him to a tree and detailed one of their number to shoot him. Luckily the man detailed was a young soldier and nervous; the bullet struck my friend in the shoulder, the Japanese ran off to rejoin his fellows, and my friend was released later by his own men. He urged me most seriously not to let myself be taken by the Japanese at this stage of the war.

I reached Kandy on the ominous date of Friday, 13th July and spent the week-end in that delightful mountain capital. The morning after my arrival I had an interview with Brigadier John Anstey, the senior officer, who endorsed with enthusiasm my request to drop into Siam; he pointed out that the campaign in Burma was drawing to its close, and when the great attack was mounted against Singapore and Malaya S.O.E. would have a vital operational role to play in Siam, through which country ran all the Japanese lines of communication with French Indo-China. Although, under Japanese military pressure, Siam had declared war on Britain, there was strong anti-Japanese feeling in the country, and many high officials and officers of the three armed services were secretly working for the Allies. A guerrilla organization, known as the 'Free Thais', was already in existence and British officers were required to train and arm these irregulars and prepare airstrips and dropping grounds in the jungle.

The Siamese Country Section was in Calcutta, where I should probably find Smiley. He had been dropped into north-east Siam in the last days of

May, but had been terribly burnt three weeks later by the premature explosion of one of S.O.E.'s new toys—an incendiary brief-case designed to burst into flames and destroy the documents inside in the event of enemy ambush or surprise; Smiley was packing documents into it when there was a short-circuit and five pounds of blazing thermite spread all over him. For a week he lay in agony, unable to sleep, with first-, second- and third-degree burns and a hole in one arm full of maggots; he was, of course, without medical attention. At last he was picked up by an aircraft of the Siamese Air Force and taken to an airstrip, where a Dakota landed and flew him to Calcutta. By now he should be nearly well enough to return to the field.

Among the brigadier's staff officers at dinner that evening I found an old friend, Major Alan Hare, who had distinguished himself in Albania during the terrible winter of 1943-4; he had emerged with severe injuries from frostbite and the immediate award of the M.C. for outstanding initiative and courage. Like myself he was part of the *Drang nach Osten* by S.O.E. officers that had followed hard upon the end of the war in Europe.

There was a curious incident before dinner. While we were having drinks on the palm-thatched veranda I was talking to Wing-Commander Redding, who used to run our Air Transport Section in Baker Street; suddenly I heard a faint plop and saw with horror that a gigantic black scorpion had fallen from the roof on to his head. With commendable presence of mind he jerked his neck smartly, so that it fell on to his shoulder, whence he brushed it to the floor. A young bull terrier and a small black puppy made a concerted dive at it, and were only just restrained in time from rushing to certain death when somebody inverted a half-pint tumbler over the creature; the glass was barely wide enough to contain it. The officer with whom I shared a hut at the training camp a few days later had an even greater shock when he found a Russell's viper in his shirt.

In the holding and training camp on the plains near Colombo where I was sent to await an aircraft for Calcutta I found a wide variety of races, white, brown and yellow; there were British, French and Dutch officers; there were Javanese, Siamese, Burmans, Karens and Gurkhas, and there were Malayan Chinese and Annamites, all waiting or training for operations by parachute, submarine or canoe. I spent my time trying, unsuccessfully, to learn a little Siamese; listening to blood-curdling lectures by the Medical Officer on the treatment of malaria, cholera, typhus, smallpox, snake-bite and syphilis; and politely declining offers to send me on a jungle-training exercise, carrying a fifty-pound rucksack. A heavy rucksack, I told the training staff, was a white man's burden that I was not prepared to tote; a small haversack such as had served me well in Albania and Poland was the most I would allow to aggravate my prickly heat; anything bulkier must be carried by mule, pony, bullock-cart or local labour—or abandoned. I never had cause to change this view.

It was almost the end of July when I reached Calcutta, arriving in that ugly fetid city on a sticky evening at the height of the monsoon. In the office of the Siamese Country Section—two stifling, noisy rooms in a dingy house on a dusty street full of pot-holes—I was received without enthusiasm by a sweaty, irritable and overworked staff officer; his appearance, like my own, was in squalid contrast to the cool serenity of the neat, pretty young secretaries who flitted in and out among the desks and the clattering typewriters. Smiley, it seemed, had gone to Simla to finish his convalescence at Viceregal Lodge as the guest of his friends the Wavells; I had better find myself a billet in the Transit Hotel until he returned—and now would I kindly get the hell out of the office and keep out of everyone's way.

This discouraging welcome, not unusual in my experience of reporting for duty in a strange theatre of war, left me nettled but not unduly depressed; for in the same office I met another old friend from Albania, John Hibberdine, a young Captain of the Cameronians who had been my close companion during the gloomy and hazardous days of my reconnaissance of the marches of Kossovo. After my departure for Montenegro early in 1944, Hibberdine had suffered appalling hardship and danger, being chased across north Albania in a series of determined German drives aimed at clearing the country of British Liaison Officers; while lying up in the inhospitable forests of Mirdita he had contracted typhoid, which all but killed him; eventually his companions managed to carry him to the coast, where an M.T.B. took him to Italy. His experiences seemed to have made little impression either on his health or his resolution; for now he was waiting to drop into southern Siam, to the Isthmus of Kra on the Burmese and Malayan borders. In his urbanely cynical company I spent the next two days exploring the restaurants and clubs of Calcutta. The European business community, we noticed, while extending to us the privilege of membership of their clubs, viewed our uniforms with a mixture of resentment and contempt which, as newcomers, we found hard to understand; at times we wondered if they would have preferred the Japanese.

Forty-eight hours after my arrival I received an urgent summons from Smiley to go to Simla to discuss plans. It was accompanied by an invitation from Lady Wavell to stay at Viceregal Lodge. I flew to Delhi and reached Simla on the morning of 3rd August. The next five days were among the happiest of my life. Although the marks of his burns were terribly evident, Smiley had made an astonishing recovery; strolling among the dark green, fir-covered hills, with the gigantic Himalayan snows nacreous and opalescent on the distant skyline, we planned in eager detail the course of our future operations in the field.

We very nearly did not get into the field. The bomb on Hiroshima shattered our pleasant pipe-dream and sent us scurrying back to Calcutta as soon as Smiley had been passed fit by a medical board. We heard the news at luncheon from a very sweet old lady, the wife of a distinguished lawyer.

'*Isn't* it wonderful?' she beamed. 'They've dropped a bomb on Japan which has the force of *ten thousand* tons of high explosive! Isn't science *marvellous*? Truly civilization progresses from day to day!'

I could only recall the bitter words of Colin Ellis's epigram:

> 'Science finds out ingenious ways to kill
> Strong men, and keep alive the weak and ill,
> That these asickly progeny may breed:
> Too poor to tax, too numerous to feed.'

It is fair to add that five years later I was to owe to science my own recovery from tuberculosis.

We did not have to linger long in Calcutta. Because of the prevailing uncertainty the Siamese Country Section decided to send in its operational parties as fast as possible. Smiley, now a lieutenant-colonel, left immediately in a Dakota that was going to land on the Siamese airstrip from which he had been flown out the previous month; with him went Brigadier Victor Jaques, commanding all Force 136 Missions in Siam. Jaques was a lawyer who had practised in Bangkok before the war; he had continued to live there during the Japanese occupation, sheltered by the Regent in his palace, where, under the noses of the enemy, he had maintained wireless communication with Calcutta and built up a subversive organization inside the country.

I was delighted to learn that I was to drop in with an old friend, Major Rowland Winn, 8th Hussars, who was also joining Smiley. I had first met Winn when I was a Carlist officer and he a correspondent for the *Daily Telegraph* in Spain. The outbreak of the Civil War found him in Madrid, but his dispatches on events there during the first few weeks were too candid for the liking of the Republican authorities, who clapped him into gaol and sentenced him to death; his life was saved by the intervention of the British Chargé d'Affaires, but he judged it prudent thereafter to report the war from the Nationalist side. In the winter of 1943 he parachuted into Albania, breaking a leg on landing; for a month, until a doctor could reach him, he lay in great pain in a shepherd's hut among the wild mountains of Cermenikë.

He held the strongest convictions on most matters of importance, especially on the subject of bullfighting, and would defend his ideas with a pugnacity in argument that was only matched by his courage in the field; a generous and loyal friend, he possessed a keen wit that made him an excellent companion and a devastating critic.

Short and stocky, with a pronounced limp from his parachute accident, he showed in his personal appearance a remarkable blend of fastidiousness and neglect; thus he seldom brushed his hair, but neither in Albania nor in

Siam was he ever without a bottle of Trumpet's after-shaving lotion. His independence of dress and manner sometimes shocked more orthodox soldiers. Just before the end of the European War he was stationed at a holding camp near Virginia Water, waiting to be sent on an operation into western Germany: bored with the inactivity of the camp he went to London for a few days' relaxation; he omitted the formality of asking permission, but left a note for the Brigadier:

> As there is nothing for me to do here I am proceeding to London. If required for operations I can be found at the Cavalry Club.

I was taking no wireless, but Winn had a set and a first-class operator, the amiable Sergeant Lawson, usually known as 'Spider', a light-hearted young man who had served with S.O.E. in Greece; he was also taking an interpreter, a giggly little Siamese, friendly, intelligent and helpful, whose *nom-de-guerre* was Toy. We left just forty-eight hours after Smiley, in a Liberator christened Vernon the Villain; it was to be a daylight drop, and so we took off at 11.30 in the morning. I was in poor shape, suffering from a mild attack of bacillary dysentery and a slight recurrence of the malaria I had contracted in Albania. However, a kindly R.A.F. doctor on the airfield dosed me heavily with sulphonamides and mepacrine, and during the flight Winn generously poured down my throat the entire contents of a flask of Courvoisier which he had brought from Europe and had saved up to drink in celebration of his arrival in Siam; his Christian action not only mitigated the squalor and discomfort of dysentery in an aircraft that had no lavatory, but took my mind off the hazards of monsoon flying among cumulonimbus clouds that could—and sometimes did—tear an aircraft apart.[1]

We flew over the Bay of Bengal, turned east near Akyab and crossed the jungle-covered hills that separate Burma from Siam.

Our dropping zone was in the north-east, near Sakon Nakorn, a town about fifty miles west of the Mekong river, which forms the frontier between Siam and French Indo-China; the area is covered in forest. At six in the evening we were over the target, and in the clear light we soon picked up the smoke signals on the dropping ground; we put on our parachutes and prepared to jump.

'Jump' is not really the right word, for since my last drop a new way of leaving the aircraft had been invented; this was a wooden chute, similar to those in swimming pools, which was lowered from the roof of the fuselage to the exit aperture. When the red light flashed 'Action Stations' the

---

[1] Our missions in Siam owed much to these aircrews, who were for long our only means of supply and who flew in the most frightening weather conditions and across the most dangerous mountain country in order to deliver our stores.

parachutist swung his legs into the trough and lay on his back with his hands gripping the sides; when he received the order to go he simply brought his hands together on his chest and, helped by a push from the dispatcher, slid down the chute and out of the hole.

We were dropping in pairs; first Winn and Lawson, and then, on the next run, Toy and myself. When we had dropped our load of containers and packages Winn took up his position on the slide. I noticed that his lips were moving as though in prayer; he caught my eye and, thinking that he might have some last message for me, I bent down to listen. He was in fact intoning Noël Coward's refrain:

In the mangrove swamps where the python romps
There is peace from ten till two.
Even caribous lie around and snooze
—There's nothing else to do

The light flashed green and he slid away, mumbling the next verse.

When it came to our turn, a few minutes later, I waited until Toy's head had disappeared before releasing my hold and laying my hands on my chest; it was all I could do to keep them there during the next two or three seconds. Then I was clear of the exit and swinging gently in mid-air with an acute pain in my crotch, which had taken most of the strain as the parachute opened. Having satisfied myself that I was not irreparably damaged I turned my attention to the ground; for a nasty moment I thought I was going to hit the roof of a wooden hut, but I missed it and landed with a great splash in a paddy-field. Soaked to the skin and temporarily blinded by mud and water, I was helped to my feet and out of my harness by three Siamese. Looking around, I was rewarded by the spectacle of Major the Honourable Rowland Winn, spattered all over with mud and paddy stalk, standing erect while he adjusted with infinite care the green and gold forage cap of the 8th Hussars which he had pulled from inside his bush shirt.

He introduced me to the leader of the reception committee, a handsome young Siamese policeman who, under the pseudonym of Kong, held a captain's commission in the British Army. Kong led us to the hut on whose roof I had so nearly landed, where the packages and containers were now assembled.

'Please sort out your kit as quickly as possible,' he asked us, speaking in quick, jerky sentences. 'We ride from here ten kilometres through the forest. There are Japanese around; their patrols are very active still, and last night they burnt a village only a mile away.'

Mounted on small, sturdy ponies we rode across the paddy towards the forest; the four of us, accompanied by Kong and another Siamese, went ahead while the rest followed with our kit. These Siamese ponies—all of them were stallions because, so Smiley told us later, it was considered bad form to ride a mare—moved like Andalusian horses, with a curious gait that was a blend of walk, trot and gallop. They went at a surprisingly fast pace and, for a short person, were comfortable to ride; but my long legs reached almost to the ground and, when I forgot to keep them clear of the pony's feet, received some painful kicks.

It was already dark when we entered the forest, but the half moon shining through the trees cast a pale, dappled light on the muddy track that wound through the tangled undergrowth. Our horses splashed, and sometimes swam, through deep pools and across swollen streams; once we crossed a creek on a wooden bridge whose posts and railings alone showed above the water, and once we swam a broad river. Twice only did we halt: when the unhappy Lawson was thrown from his pony into a dark and slimy puddle, and when Winn's forage cap was swept off by an overhanging branch. Otherwise we rode in silence at a steady pace, inhaling the heavy, scented warmth of the sodden forest while glow-worms and fireflies flashed in the misty darkness; at intervals the rain showered upon us, cool and soothing.

It was nearly ten o'clock when we arrived at the village of Akat, where we were to spend the night. At the point where the path debouched into the clearing we found the headman awaiting us surrounded by a curious and whispering crowd of men and women carrying lighted brushwood torches; joining the palms of his hands before him he bowed us a graceful welcome. He led us to a long, narrow building raised on wooden piles to a height of twelve or fifteen feet above the ground and approached by a flight of steps leading to an open veranda. This was the school-house, where we were going to sleep.

In construction and design it resembled many other houses in northeastern Siam. From the veranda we passed into a large room, bare of furniture except for a table and benches down the centre; the table was laid for a meal and mattresses were spread against one of the walls. The floor was spotlessly clean, the boards scrubbed almost to a polish. Food was set before us—cold boiled rice with pieces of chicken, meat balls, eggs and chilies; also a bottle of what Kong called 'Siamese whisky'—a potent rice spirit with a sour, not unpleasing flavour. Already comatose from illness and fatigue I could not bring myself to eat or drink more than the mouthful that politeness demanded; the effects of the doctor's pills and Winn's brandy had long worn off, leaving me weak and sick and feverish. During the last hour of the journey I had been barely conscious, and at the end I had been unable to dismount without help. Winn and Lawson undressed me, laid me on a mattress and heaped blankets upon my shivering, sweating body.

We rested all next day; by the evening, although still weak from loss of blood, I was beginning to recover. The following morning we left Akat and rode all day through the forest, keeping up a fast pace along a broad but marshy track; we spent the night in a village with the charming name of Ba Wa, where a squad of guerrillas, lined up in front of the school, greeted us with a shout of '*Knio!*', repeated three times, and a smart present arms. They carried British service rifles and looked keen and fit.

We made an early start and covered ten miles before breakfast and another ten before noon; then we came to a wide expanse of water, a river in flood, where *pirogues* awaited us—hollowed tree-trunks, each one a masterpiece of skilful workmanship. We were paddled silently over the surface of the water, the half-submerged forest around us reminding me of pictures I had seen of the Florida Everglades; after two miles we landed at a house beside the water and had lunch.

Kong had received a message from Smiley saying that a lorry would be awaiting us that afternoon about a mile from this house; while we rested he sent a scout to look for it. I reflected that, whether or not the Japanese surrendered, we should be pretty safe from them as long as we stayed in the forest. Our Siamese friends made extensive use of scouts, and their intelligence systems seemed excellent; we ought to have plenty of warning of Japanese movements, and in this vast area of forest we should have no difficulty in hiding.

Kong's scout returned to say that the lorry was waiting. We set off on foot, but mid-afternoon in the tropics is not a good time for a walk, especially during the monsoon; and so, when an old man driving a bullock cart offered us a lift we climbed up thankfully beside him. Our escort of guerrillas trudged along on either side, apparently quite content.

We found Smiley's truck, a bright red Chevrolet, parked beside a rough track that ran from the verge of the forest through a wide expanse of waterlogged paddy-field. We climbed into the back, where we were soon joined by the twenty men of our escort, and tried to stave off bruises and abrasions as the vehicle lurched and plunged in the ruts and pot-holes. At length we came on to the straight, brick-coloured *piste* that was the road between Sakon Nakorn and Udaun; Japanese military transport used this road and police patrols were frequent, and so our guards made us lie on the floor and covered us with a tarpaulin. After a quarter of an hour the lorry stopped and we were allowed to emerge from hiding, sweaty and half-suffocated. We were hustled off the road on to a forest track, which led us in a few moments to another village with an enchanting name—Phannikom. There we found Smiley with his wireless operator, Sergeant Collins, and a wiry, lightly built Siamese with a gaunt, tormented face, whom Smiley introduced to me as Pluto.

I had already heard of this man. Tiang Sirikhand, alias Pluto, was one of the founders of the Free Thai movement and its leader in north-eastern Siam, where he had been born of an influential family about thirty-five years before.

Parliamentary Deputy for Sakon Nakorn, close friend and staunch supporter of the Regent, Pridi Panomyong, he had given valuable service to the Allies and in particular to Smiley, who liked and admired him for his kindness, competence and integrity. He was a forceful if humourless personality, with great powers of organization and leadership; his enemies accused him of Communist sympathies, I think unfairly.[1]

His grim, swarthy face relaxed in a smile of unusual warmth and charm as he greeted us and, turning to me, remarked:

'Smiley tells me it is your birthday today. We have arranged a celebration for you.'

In the excitement and fatigue of the last few days I had forgotten that this was indeed my thirtieth birthday, 19th August 1945.

It was now about four o'clock. Over mugs of tea we discussed plans for the future. Although it seemed likely that the war was coming to an end there had as yet been no surrender, and we could not be sure of the reactions of local Japanese commanders if we should fall into their hands; there were some grim rumours of the fate of British officers in Burma who had been captured in the last few days. We knew that the enemy had been preparing a drive against this area, and it was still possible that they might launch an attack on the guerrillas—although they would find it hard to catch us in these miles of forest, where our men knew every path. Calcutta's instructions were that we should remain underground until we received the code word 'Goldfish', authorizing us to approach the Japanese.

'Meanwhile,' Smiley continued, 'I want you, Rowly, to go to Naung Khai, north-west of here, and Peter to go to Nakorn Panom, to the east. Both towns are on the Mekong river, which, as you know, forms the frontier between Siam and the province of Laos in Indo-China; each is the capital of a *changvad* or province. You'll meet the two Provincial Governors here tonight and leave with them tomorrow; I myself am going to Sakon Nakorn with Pluto. Peter, you'll be the worst off, having no wireless contact; but Calcutta have promised to drop in a set and operator for you as soon as they can.'

'I'm afraid that, until we get orders from Calcutta, I can only give you the vaguest instructions. Find out all you can about your districts, and about the places across the river in Laos—that means Vientiane for Rowly, and for

---

[1] *The Times* of 6th January 1955 carried a report from its Bangkok correspondent to the effect that Nai Tiang Sirikhand, who was described as a 'well-known Communist sympathizer', was organizing an 'army of liberation' of Siamese in northern Laos and that he was receiving Viet-minh support. On the other hand, his close friend, General Phoumi Nosavan, the Laotian anti-Communist leader, recently assured me that Pluto was no Communist. The question, alas, is now purely academic, for Pluto himself was murdered in Siam a few years ago, allegedly on the orders of the Chief of Police, General Phao.

Peter Thakhek and Savannakhet farther south; especially get all the dope you can about Japanese and prisoners of war. We can keep in touch through the Siamese, who can be trusted not to open our letters—unlike the Albanian Partisans!'

At seven o'clock, after toasting our reunion with a few whiskies, we walked over to the school-house for my birthday party. If I describe it in detail this is because it was typical of almost every party I attended in north-east Siam—and they were many, for the Siamese are a friendly and laughter-loving people. A great crowd of men and girls was gathered there to greet us and a roar of welcome hailed our entry into the large classroom, where long tables loaded with food and drink displayed the magnificence of Siamese hospitality. Seeing the roast sucking pigs, ducks, chickens, plates heaped with meat, vegetables and fruit, and the huge tureens of rice I found it hard to believe that we were in a small village in a rain-soaked tropical forest.

Before dining we were led out on to the veranda, where stood several great earthenware jars filled with rice beer; a thick layer of rice floated on the top of each jar and from each protruded several thin bamboo drinking straws; the jars were colloquially known as *changs* (elephants) and the bamboos were their tusks. All this we were told by Pluto, who, beaming with enthusiasm, made us drink plentifully from each *chang*; the beer tasted slightly sweet and deceptively mild.

On the veranda, also, we met the Governors of Naung Khai and Nakorn Panom. The former was small and slightly built with an impressively quiet but friendly manner; the latter, named Ta Win, was taller, broader, stouter and more effusive than his colleague. He had very thick lips and an excited, bubbly way of speaking. Although he knew a little English, he had with him his interpreter, Sang-a, an emaciated little man with a hoarse, nervous giggle and a twitch, a man who seemed to me a little too anxious to please everyone.

We dined standing at the tables, as at a buffet, and helping ourselves. There was a remarkable variety of food; in addition to what I have mentioned there was pork, water buffalo, barking deer, fish, eels, snails, frogs, bamboo shoots, coconuts and every kind of tropical fruit; and there were small dishes of a chili sauce so powerful that anything flavoured with it turned to fire in the mouth.

While we were eating, girls brought us glasses of *lao kao*, a fierce rice spirit, which they offered with a charming little bow. As soon as our glasses were empty they were refilled, the girls taking it in turns to serve each of us; Siamese women are uncommonly pretty, and in the face of their bewitching smiles and mischievous dark eyes I found myself unable to refuse, with the result that my head was swimming and my eyes were a trifle glazed by the end of the meal. It was foolish of me, so soon after dysentery, to drink so much; but the warmth of my welcome made me forget my illness.

When we had finished we were led to a row of chairs at one end of the room; more *changs* were placed in front of us, from which we were continually pressed to drink. The tables were removed, and an orchestra assembled to play Siamese tunes for us on stringed instruments and what looked like large bamboo pan-pipes. The notes were sweet and pure and the music had, to our western ears, an attractive if somewhat monotonous melody. Local folk-songs followed, Then, to my horror, Pluto called for a song from each of us; worse still, as the guest of honour I had to start. Smiley urged me to sing something Polish, and so, in a voice hoarse with *lao kao* and thick with rice beer, I gave them the Warszawianka, explaining with alcoholic exuberance that it was a song of revolution against a foreign oppressor. My performance met with courteous applause from the Siamese and hoots of ribald laughter from our party.

Then began the Siamese national dance known as Ramwong, in which partners shuffle round the room in a double line, moving arms and hands to a slow, sinuous rhythm. It was a joy to watch the beautiful figures and graceful gestures of the Siamese girls, but when we were asked to join in, even my well-fortified spirit quailed; Smiley by constant practice had become quite competent, but personally I felt I resembled an inebriated camel slowly swaying its neck and limbs from side to side. Sergeant Lawson, however, was troubled by no such inhibitions; he whirled round the room like a dervish, arms and legs flying, and so much did he delight our hosts that for a while he held the floor alone.

I suffered no more than a hangover for that night's intoxication. Smiley comforted me.

'Don't worry. You're pretty well expected to get plastered on these occasions. Even I have been carried home to bed.'

II

'A FATE WORSE THAN KEMP'

The inhabitants of the fifteen provinces of north-east Siam differ from those of the rest of the country in that they have close ties of race and language with the Laotians beyond the Mekong. Although a little impatient of the authority of Bangkok and of the civil servants sent from there to administer them they had, and I believe still have, no inclination towards separatism;[1] commerce with Laos, however, is frequent and virtually unrestricted.

The area is a plateau averaging live hundred feet above sea-level, most of it covered in forest of a type which geographers call 'dry monsoon forest' and the Siamese call *padeng*; this forest assumes in the dry season a stark and lifeless appearance because the trees shed their foliage and only the undergrowth retains a certain tarnished green. It is for the most part a forlorn and desolate region, whether sodden under the monsoon rains or dusty and desiccated in the winter months, monotonous to the eye, with scarcely a break in the colourless forest landscape save for the few acres of paddy-fields near the villages. Only under bright moonlight have I seen it beautiful.

The soil is poor and so, therefore, are the people, who supplement their income by breeding water buffalo, oxen and pigs for export to other parts of the country. But poverty has not brought discontent; most of the land is owned by the peasants who till it, and those twin vultures, the absentee landlord and the money-lender, cannot prey here as in India and in Lower Siam.

All but three per cent of the population live in villages, most of which lie some distance from the road and are approached by torturous tracks through the forest.

> Their villages, surrounded with bright green ricefields, are built in the thick shade of lofty mango trees, groves of bamboo and coconut palms. The wooden houses are on stilts, with cattle and water buffalo often living under them. Almost every village has a Wat, which is a Buddhist religious enclosure containing a temple, a pavilion, and a

---

[1] See an excellent article on north-east Siam by Professor Charles Madge in *The Times* of 7th January 1955, to which I am much indebted. But Pluto had to flee from Siam in 1949, accused of attempting to form a separate state in the north-east (*The Times*, 6th January 1955).

residence for the monks. The village communities are socially homogenous and in their easy-going way they hang together and help each other. There are no divisions of religion, caste or language. The position of women is traditionally good and family life is traditionally happy and united.[1]

One object of hatred these people shared with their Laotian cousins; the Annamese. Indeed, Smiley told me that Pluto's guerrillas shot any Annamite they caught, suspecting him, often with good reason, of spying for the Japanese.[2] There were Annamese colonies in many towns of the north-east; in Nakorn Panom they had their separate village. The Chinese, on the other hand, though not loved were tolerated; they owned all the hotels and eating houses and, together with the Indians, all the shops.

Such was the land in which for the next five months I was to make my home.

Nakorn Panom was a clean-looking little town, consisting of a muddy main street, lined on either side with shops and running north and south beside the Mekong, and a few small side streets leading down to the river or dwindling away westwards into country tracks. To the west the ground rose gently from the river bank and the town, past open fields and scattered houses to a small landing strip on the verge of the forest; on the other two sides were banana plantations and coconut palms. The Wat lay half a mile to the south; about the same distance to the north lived the Annamese, earning their livelihood chiefly on the river. There was one hotel, owned of course by Chinese.

I arrived at half past five on the evening of 20th August in a rickety old bus with Governor Ta Win, Sang-a and a small party of guerrillas. On the way from Phannikom we had passed several lorries full of Japanese troops, who had paid no attention to us, looking straight ahead with blank, unseeing faces.

Among my companions on this journey was a lean, handsome Lao of about twenty-five, with a very soft voice and an unusually charming smile. He told me that he had been in charge of what he called the 'Free Lao' resistance against the Japanese in the Savannakhet area; what he did not tell me was that he was on his way back there to organize a similar resistance movement against the French. His name, which he gave simply as Phoumi, meant nothing to me at the time, and it was more that fifteen years before I

---

[1] Professor Madge, op. cit.

[2] It should not be forgotten that President Ho Chi Minh, like President Sukarno of Indonesia, was awarded a high decoration by the Japanese.

was to see him again. Now he is the most powerful figure in Laos and the bitterest enemy of his former allies the Viet-minh.

We turned left in the main street and bumped slowly through the pot-holes, past the stucco fronts of the Governor's office and 'Flail of Justice' to the Governor's house, a yellow, plaster-fronted, two-storey building in European style, with a cool green garden shaded by coconut palms. It faced on to the Mekong, at this season nearly a mile wide and flowing swiftly over hidden sandbanks in a series of swirling eddies and whirlpools. On the other side the white houses of Thakhek showed clearly, picked out amid a blaze of green. Behind them rose the first ranges of the Chaine Annamitique—dark, jungle-covered mountains, grim and threatening, their summits swathed in black, grey-streaked clouds, lit at intervals by jagged, purple flashes of lightning; the thunder rolled to our ears across the mud-brown river.

The following day passed uneventfully. The Governor, who seemed to think I was a confirmed alcoholic, produced throughout the day a succession of strange new drinks for me to sample; with the exception of a light golden rum from Indo-China they were all disgusting. In the afternoon he took me to the club, where I met the local officials; the Deputy Governor, the Police Captain and Lieutenant, the Sheriff, Harbourmaster, Chief Customs Officer, Doctor, and a quiet, shy little man who astonished me by introducing himself as 'the Director of Humanity'. He turned out to be the schoolmaster.

Japanese troops seldom came to Nakorn Panom—only when crossing to or from Thakhek; we should have plenty of warning of their approach, and there was a company of our guerrillas in the town. On the second day after my arrival the Governor thought it would be safe for me to set up my own headquarters. The place he had prepared was known as the Officials' Rest House, a large bungalow on the open, rising ground behind the town, like all Government buildings it had walls of cream-washed laterite; a wide, cool veranda led to a long dining-room and several bedrooms. The house backed on to the airfield. Commanding a wide view across the town and river to Thakhek and the mountains of Laos it was an ideal headquarters. I moved in there the same evening. I was given a staff of servants, assisted by convicts from the local prison, to see to my comfort, and a guard of two police and four guerrillas to ensure my safety.

During my first week I was able to gain some idea of the situation on the other side of the river. I sent agents to Thakhek, men who had relatives over there; and I drove with Governor Ta Win to Mukdahan, some fifty miles south of Nakorn Panom, to brief others to bring me news from Savannakhet. My inquiries established that there was in Thakhek a number of French civilian internees but no prisoners of war; that there was a force of French and Laotian guerrillas living in the jungle south of Thakhek, commanded by a certain Lieutenant Tavernier; that there was a similar force near

Savannakhet under a Lieutenant Quinquenel, and that all were in urgent need of food, money and medical supplies. I received also a great deal of information that turned out to be false. The problem of sifting true from inaccurate reports was one that I was never able to solve the whole time I was on the frontier; I was at the mercy of my agents, who turned out as often as not to be double agents.

This question of double agents became more difficult when the struggle began between the French and the Viet-minh, because the Siamese, on whose advice I was largely dependent for my recruiting, were hostile to the French cause.

My most disastrous experiment was in October, with an Indian agent—a Sikh merchant who was well recommended to me. The day after I had recruited him and given him his instructions, together with a sizeable sum of money, I received a signal from our office in Bangkok, ordering me to arrest him as an ex-agent of the Japanese; before I could do so he had disappeared.

I was soon obliged to disobey my orders to stay underground. On 25th August the Police Lieutenant brought me a message that two Frenchmen in Thakhek had been condemned to death by the Japanese and were about to be executed. To save their lives I felt I must act at once. Calling on the Governor I asked him for transport across to Thakhek, intending to present myself to the Japanese commander, a Captain Nakajima, and dissuade him from carrying out the sentence. The Governor and the Police Captain, who was with him, implored me not to go; almost in tears they protested that if anything happened to me the consequences to themselves, and perhaps to their country, would be disastrous. I could, they pointed out, achieve as much and probably more through a letter, which they promised to deliver in Thakhek immediately.

Their arguments seemed reasonable, and so I abandoned my original idea—not unwillingly, I may add. Instead, I wrote to Captain Nakajima, warning him that he would be held personally responsible for the safety of his prisoners, and asking to be allowed to visit them. The Governor added a letter of his own. He agreed that if we did not receive a satisfactory reply by the following morning I might go in person. I also relayed the news to Smiley, who had moved from Sakon Nakorn to Ubon, about 150 miles down the Mekong.

I spent an anxious day. About seven o'clock in the evening I was sitting on my veranda watching the green and lilac colours on the hills of Laos deepen to purple and indigo in the twilight; at intervals the cackle of a gekko lizard on the ceiling broke in upon the stillness to jar the rhythm of my thoughts. I sprang eagerly to my feet as the Police Lieutenant approached with the two messengers who had delivered my letter to Thakhek. They brought me an answer from Captain Nakajima, written in good English and courteously phrased, regretting that until he received instructions from his superiors he must decline my request for an interview and for the release of the prisoners; but he assured me that in the meantime they would come to no harm. After a further exchange of letters, in which I was joined by Smiley, who paid me a visit the next day, the two condemned men were released from close arrest.

Dining with the Governor one evening I met the American Dr. Holliday, a Presbyterian missionary who had lived in Siam for fifteen years before the war, and previously for thirteen years in China. Having left the country before the Japanese occupation he had been dropped back there in April to form an intelligence network for the American O.S.S., and he now held the rank of major in the U.S. Army. He was one of the very few O.S.S. officers in Siam, this theatre of operations being the agreed responsibility of the British South-East Asia Command. A stocky, well-built man in the early fifties, with a bronzed square face, a strong jaw and a quiet, friendly manner, he was held in great affection and respect by the Siamese people, whose language he spoke fluently.

He explained to me the reason behind the Governor's anxiety that I should not cross the river.

'These people are terribly afraid for their independence. They feel they're in bad with the Allies—even though it wasn't their fault they were sold out to the Nips. They are responsible for your safety and they think that if at this critical time something should happen to you, or to any British officer in Thailand, they would lose their independence.'

'But surely if I put it in writing that I take full responsibility myself, that I've gone against their advice . . . ?'

'That makes no difference. They still feel they would be blamed.'

It was becoming difficult to avoid the Japanese on my tour of the area; it also seemed unnecessary. While visiting the Sheriff of Mukdahan I was embarrassed to find myself in a street crowded with their troops. I received some dirty looks from the officers; by the men I was ignored.

On 29th August Smiley passed me the code word 'Goldfish'; on 2nd September came the news of the Japanese surrender. By that time the Japanese forces in my area had moved south to Ubon, where Smiley immediately found his hands full. Outside the town there was a large prisoner-of-war camp, full of British, Australians and Dutch. Although the efficient and tactful administration of the famous Colonel Toosey relieved him from responsibility inside the camp, Smiley had the task of receiving and sorting the daily parachute drops which supplied it, and of ensuring the smooth cooperation of the Siamese civil and military authorities which was so necessary for its welfare.

Another of his duties was to supervise the disarming of some eleven thousand Japanese and the shooting of their horses, which were in terrible condition, having been shamefully neglected by their masters. He was astonished, therefore, to see the Japanese soldiers in tears as they shot their horses, and then to watch them remove their caps and bow for two minutes before filling in the graves, which they covered with flowers.

My attention at this time was occupied almost wholly with events around Thakhek. Two days after my arrival at Nakorn Panom I had seen a Dakota flying low over the opposite bank; soon afterwards I received reports that it had dropped two French parachutists, a man and a girl. On 29th August one of my agents brought me a letter from the former, Lieutenant Klotz, addressed to 'The British Officer at Lakhon',[1] saying that he was in difficulties and would like to meet me. He suggested a rendezvous at the Catholic mission house on the island of Dong Don, a few miles north-west of Thakhek, in two days' time.

The Governor would not hear of my crossing to the island, which was not in Siamese territory; mindful of Dr. Holliday's words I did not press the point. Instead, we arranged that the Governor should take me in his launch to the village of Ban A Sa Mat, opposite Dong Don, where we could wait while the launch fetched Klotz from the island.

We started after lunch on 31st August—the Governor, Sang-a and myself, with a small escort, all bristling with Stens and carbines; even I was asked to bring my carbine, for what purpose I cannot imagine. The launch, an ancient open boat with a canvas canopy on stanchions to protect us from the broiling sun, puffed and spluttered noisily up the tawny river, making slow progress against the current. Keeping near to the bank, a steep cliff of red laterite with banana plantations and a few huts on the top, and passing close beneath the squalid dwellings of the Annamites, who stared at us with surly curiosity, we reached Ban A Sa Mat in the sweltering heat of mid-afternoon. We waited on the veranda of a hut while the launch went to find Klotz.

Half an hour later he appeared, a dark, thick-set young man of about twenty-five with strong, heavy features and a sombre expression; his speech was slow, his voice hoarse but soft, his command of English nearly perfect. By birth he was Alsatian. He was very tired.

He belonged to a French organization similar to our Force 136.

Together with his wireless operator—'who is a she', he explained—he had been dropped by the Dakota we had seen on the 22nd, into the hills about ten miles north of Thakhek.

'For the first few days we lived in a cave,' he told me. 'But now we have moved to a village. Since our arrival my operator has been unable to make contact with our base at Rangoon, although she has been trying six skeds a day. She is very disheartened. Now my hand generator is broken and I cannot recharge my batteries.

---

[1] Alternate name for Nakorn Panom.

'On the 27th I went to Thakhek—in uniform of course—to ask the Japanese to let me see the French prisoners. The Japanese commander was very correct—gave me lunch but would not let me see the prisoners. He mentioned your name, but without comment. Afterwards he drove me in a car outside the town, and I went back to my village.'

He added that there were very few Japanese left in Thakhek and none, except deserters, in the country around.

It seemed to me that Klotz would be much more comfortable, and would be able to operate more effectively, if he set up his headquarters in my house. The Governor readily agreed and promised to charge his batteries at Nakorn Panom; in any case I was expecting a wireless set very shortly. We arranged, therefore, that Klotz and his operator should join me in the course of the next few days.

We brought him back with us to dine and stay the night. Next morning we took him in the launch to Dong Don, where he had a *pirogue* waiting to ferry him back to the far side. The Governor, reassured by the news that there were no Japanese outside Thakhek, landed with us on the island. We followed a muddy, slippery track through the jungle until we came to a small Laotian village, where Klotz led us to the house of his piroguier. The young Lao lived with his mother and wife; all of them welcomed us warmly, going down on their knees to us and clasping their hands in greeting. The Governor and I had to return immediately, but for Klotz, who was staying there to eat, his host lolled a chicken, and in a manner I had never seen before. Taking a wooden crossbow from the wall he fitted to it a slim bamboo arrow. With his bow at the ready he sidled down the steps to a patch of beaten earth in front of the house, where a few hens were scratching at the soil; selecting his victim he shot it through the middle of the body. The wretched bird screeched and flapped, splashing the ground with blood, until he seized it and wrung its neck.

On 3rd September I had a message from Smiley asking me to meet him at Ubon, where he had a wireless set and operator awaiting me. There was much excitement that day, for the names of the new Siamese government had been announced. Pluto had been nominated Minister Without Portfolio; Marshal Phibul, the 'Strong Man' of the country, who had declared war against us, was under arrest, awaiting trial as a war criminal.[1]

In the evening I had a visit from a Lieutenant de Fay, one of Tavernier's officers, who commanded a group of Laotian guerrillas at Pak Hin Boun, on the Mekong above Thakhek. He gave me a very clear picture of the situation, which I was soon able to confirm for myself.

---

[1] It was not so very long before he became once more the Strong Man, and Pluto and the Regent Pridi Panomyong were fugitives. Now, of course, Marshal Sarit is the Strong Man and Phibul an exile.

Although the capital of the Laotian province of Cammon, Thakhek had a very large Annamese population, which in fact outnumbered the Laos; in the countryside, on the other hand, there were comparatively few Annamites, for they tended to congregate where there was some form of industry to give them employment. There was no love lost between the two races. The majority of Laos stood by the French, whereas the Annamites detested them and, having collaborated actively with the Japanese, were now organizing themselves into a Communist movement, with the declared intention of expelling the French from the whole of Indo-China; this movement was the Viet-minh. Now the Annamites, having obtained large supplies of arms from the Japanese, would, after the departure of the latter, control Thakhek. Tavernier's troops were too weak and poorly armed to drive them out; indeed, they would be lucky to hold their own.

Tension was increasing. The Viet-minh were mustering their forces and had already attacked isolated groups of Franco-Laotian guerrillas, protesting in the usual Communist manner that it was the French who were attacking them. Most serious of all at the moment was the position of the French internees in the town, some forty men, women and children who had been confined in the convent under Japanese guard. Now, however, Captain Nakajima had withdrawn his guards, leaving the prisoners in the care of the *Chaokhoueng*, the Laotian Governor of Cammon. This official had no means of protecting them, being himself at the mercy of the Viet-minh, whose leaders—or Delegates, as they chose to style themselves—had declared their intention of holding the internees as hostages against the French. The attitude of the Viet-minh towards these defenceless people became so menacing that one of the women wrote a letter to de Fay, which he showed me, imploring him to intervene at once.

As a Frenchman de Fay could do nothing; and I could do little enough. However, I immediately wrote to the Annamese Delegates warning them not to harm the French civilians; I gave myself the arrogant title of 'Allied Representative at Nakorn Panom', for I knew that the Viet-minh were hoping to enlist Anglo-American support. I wrote also to Captain Nakajima, asking him to put some troops at the disposal of the Chaokhoueng. Clearly the only solution would be to transport all the internees to the Siamese side of the river, where the Governor readily agreed to receive them. This was a situation which I must discuss with Smiley. I resolved to go to Ubon next day.

A message to Pluto secured me a car and driver for the journey; early the following evening I reached the large wooden bungalow on the outskirts of Ubon where Smiley had established his headquarters. Impressed with the gravity of the situation he agreed to follow me to Nakorn Panom and accompany me across the river to try and evacuate the internees.

In the morning I went with him to visit the prisoner-of-war camp. Talking to those men who had suffered so much, I was filled with admiration for

23

their high morale; for the calm, detached manner in which they talked of their years of misery, overwork and starvation and described the brutalities of their guards, particularly the Koreans—the savage beatings and the horrors of the 'water torture'. They seemed to feel no bitterness, no urge to indulge in reprisals against their former gaolers.

Among the Japanese some discipline still remained; the officers who took orders from Smiley continued to exact obedience from their men. But in the evenings there was a good deal of drunkenness among all ranks; a few days before my visit the Colonel commanding Japanese troops in Ubon, who was unpopular, was badly bitten by an intoxicated private in a brothel.

I left for Nakorn Panom after lunch, reinforced at last by a wireless set and operator and a code name with which to preface all my messages to Calcutta—'Sackcloth'. Jock Rork, the operator, was a tall, rangy, red-haired sergeant in the Royal Corps of Signals with nearly twenty years of service behind him. A man of independent, even contentious character with more than a streak of obstinacy, he was expert at his job, warm-hearted, loyal and fearless. We travelled in a three-ton lorry which Smiley had given me and reached Nakorn Panom after dark. There I found François Klotz and his operator, Edith Fournier, a cheerful, fresh-faced, buxom young woman clothed like the rest of us in olive-green battle-dress and jungle boots and wearing the badges of a second lieutenant of the French Army. They had arrived that morning.

I was awakened next day by a messenger with a letter from Captain Tavernier, written from the village of Ban Tung, about twenty miles south of Thakhek. He told me that he had been appointed civil and military governor of the province of Cammon, with the task of restoring order there as quickly as possible, and asked my help in persuading the Japanese commander in Thakhek to allow him and his troops to occupy the town immediately; to this end he suggested a meeting with me and named a village on the far bank of the Mekong, where some of his men would await me and take me to his headquarters. He also begged me to send him arms, medical supplies—especially for malaria and dysentery—and money; all of which he needed urgently.

When the Japanese occupied French Indo-China in 1940 they did so with the acquiescence of the Vichy authorities who at that time ruled the colony; the French Colonial Army had orders not to resist. Until March 1945 the Japanese were content to use the country as a base, leaving the administration in the hands of the French, whose soldiers retained their arms. But on 9th March they struck. They arrested every French official and officer they could lay hands on; and they murdered the great majority of those they caught. Pockets of the Armée Coloniale resisted and were overwhelmed. In Tonkin a large body of troops fought its way towards the Chinese border but, cut off from outside help, it suffered heavy losses from fever and dysentery and soon ceased to be an effective fighting force.

With few exceptions the Annamese units surrendered or deserted; but the Laotian troops remained loyal to their officers and went with them into the mountains or the jungle to continue resistance. Short of arms and ammunition, with little food and less medical equipment, plagued by every form of tropical disease, those gallant, great-hearted little men stood by their splendid officers and N.C.O.s, who were the flower of the French Army. Actively, they could do little against the Japanese; they could hardly remain alive. But they survived; now they meant to recover Indo-China for France.

Tavernier's needs were urgent; but more important was the danger threatening the French civilians in Thakhek. I wrote back to Tavernier, saying I would meet him as soon as our hands were free of this problem.

Smiley arrived in the afternoon. The Governor was so impressed with the necessity for action that he said he would accompany us to Thakhek in person. While he busied himself organizing food and housing for the evacuees Smiley and I drafted letters to Captain Nakajima and the *Chaokhoueng*, asking for interviews with him and with the Viet-minh Delegates. Nakajima did not answer, but next morning we received a polite note from the *Chaokhoueng* asking us to meet him at the Residency in Thakhek at two o'clock in the afternoon.

Soon after noon on 7th September we embarked in the Governor's launch—Smiley, Klotz, the Governor and myself; two Annamese servants came with us, a mechanic and a pilot. At the Residency gate, opposite the landing-stage, the *Chaokhoueng* awaited us, an unhappy little figure in a white shirt and baggy, purple silk pantaloons reaching half-way down his legs. After a brief talk, in which it became clear that the poor man was much too scared to intervene with the Viet-minh leaders, we persuaded him to take us to see his charges.

Ignoring the groups of scowling Annamites who sauntered through the streets with slung rifles, we came, after a walk of ten minutes, to the convent, a long, low, wooden building beside a white-washed chapel. A thin, fair woman of about forty came out on to the veranda to greet us; this was Madame Collin, widow of the French Resident who had been beheaded in March. She was the acknowledged spokesman of the rest by virtue not only of position but of character, for she was a woman of indestructible serenity, kindliness and courage.

We were at once surrounded by a pathetic throng of women and children, wretchedly clad in worn and shapeless garments little better than rags; they threw their arms around us, clasped and held our hands or simply stared in apathetic or bewildered disbelief. Some, in an agony of fear, called on us to protect them from the Annamese; others kept silence, only betraying by the tears that poured down their cheeks and the spasms that shook their bodies the desolation of their hearts. All of them begged for news of their husbands; we had to say we knew nothing, for we could not tell them that we believed all their men to be dead.

There were eighteen women and fourteen children—boys and girls between the ages of four and fourteen; there were five nuns, whose steadfast faith and devotion had sustained them all through the past grim months, and there were some forty Eurasian orphans whom they had taken under their care. All these lived, sleeping on the floor, in a long dormitory that had been, I think, the refectory.

Living with the priest, in a room adjoining the chapel, were three men, all civilians and very lucky to be alive. One of them, the electrician in charge of the power station, had been under sentence of death. On 22nd August the Dakota which dropped Klotz had flown over Thakhek to drop leaflets. The electrician unwisely waved to it, was seen by an Annamite and reported to the Japanese; that evening he was arrested, together with his wife and child, and taken by car to the fourth kilometre stone on the road south of the town. Realizing that they were going to be executed he warned his family to run for safety as soon as the car drew up; they leaped out and ran towards the jungle but the woman and child were quickly recaptured and shot. They were buried beside the kilometre stone. He himself wandered for two days in the forest until, driven by hunger and exhaustion, he approached the hut of an Annamese charcoal-burner and begged for help; the Annamite, after hacking him about the arms with a machete, handed him over to the Japanese, who were going to kill him when our letters reached Captain Nakajima. The slashes on his arms were open to the bone.

'I think, gentlemen, you have only just arrived in time,' said Madame Collin in her quiet voice. 'The Annamite guards who have replaced the Japanese have become extremely menacing. They show us their knives and make gestures of cutting our throats.'

We looked across the courtyard to the gateway, where a group of villainous-looking young men in grey topees squatted in the dust, their rifles between their knees, while others wandered up and down casting furtive glances in our direction.

'We'll go and see the Annamese Delegates now,' announced Smiley. 'Then we'll take all these people across to Nakorn Panom tonight.'

While he and Klotz were conducted to the Delegates, and the Chaokhoueng and Governor Ta Win went to the quay to organize boats and crews for the evacuation, I stayed at the convent in case the guards should take advantage of their absence to make trouble.

It was two hours, and nearly dusk, before Smiley returned to say that all was ready. He and Klotz had had a stormy session, alternately cajoling and threatening the Delegates, who had protested vehemently against this interference and had raised the astonishing argument that France was not a signatory to the Peace Treaty. But at length Smiley had overridden their objections, and now everything was prepared for the move; the Governor awaited us by the river.

Under the direction of Madame Collin and the nuns the packing began in a bustle of excitement and relief. Suddenly there was an interruption: we heard a bark of orders as a Japanese patrol marched through the gate and halted beneath the veranda. An N.C.O. beckoned to Smiley, Klotz and me. As we reached the bottom of the steps, the patrol fell in on either side of us and at an order marched us away amid the despairing wails of the women. We turned and waved to them, shouting that we should soon return, but the Japanese jammed their rifles in our backs and snarled at us to keep moving. Several of them were obviously drunk.

We were marched to a house on the waterfront, up a flight of stairs and into a bare room furnished only with a desk, at which sat a young Japanese captain with straight, dark hair and a handsome, strangely Latin cast of face. He bowed to us and introduced himself as Captain Nakajima. In jerky, broken English he explained that he had not yet received the precise terms of the surrender treaty, and that without orders from his superiors he could not let us evacuate the French civilians.

Angrily we protested against the manner of our arrest and the behaviour of his patrol. Smiling thinly, the captain apologized and promised that the offending soldiers would be punished; but, although he would place no further restriction on our movements, he bluntly refused to let us remove the French. Smiley undertook to get him the necessary orders from the Japanese colonel at Ubon; meanwhile he demanded that the Annamese guards at the convent should be replaced at once by Japanese, and that the captain should hold himself responsible for the safety of its inmates. Nakajima agreed and, while we waited, detailed the guards and ordered them to escort us back. Gravely he bowed us out.

'Obviously,' growled Smiley, 'he's been tipped off by the Annamese and is scared of them because they outnumber his men.'

Back at the convent we watched the mounting of the Japanese guard and the expulsion of the Annamese, who left with surprising docility. But our troubles were not yet over. A commotion on the veranda brought us running, to find a drunken Japanese soldier trying to tear a wrist watch off one of the nuns. Smiley, who arrived first, tried to remonstrate with him, whereupon the Japanese, an ugly look on his face, drew his bayonet; I felt for my pistol. At that moment the Corporal of the Guard walked up to us, took the soldier by the arm and spun him round, hissing at him angrily; the soldier lurched and muttered, but the corporal slapped his face and continued to slap until the man staggered away, grunting.

'Stay here,' ordered Smiley, 'I'm going back to report this to the captain.'

A quarter of an hour later he returned with a grim-faced Nakajima and another patrol; the offending soldier, after a further bout of slapping, was marched away, his place being taken by an evidently sober guard. Smiley and Klotz returned to Nakorn Panom, the former on his way to Ubon to secure the necessary authority for the release of the refugees, the latter to ask Calcutta for an immediate drop of food, clothing and medical supplies on my airfield. I remained in the convent—where I stayed with the priest, who opened two bottles of his Communion wine in my honour—in order to reassure the refugees; or, as Rowland Winn described it in a subsequent signal, 'to protect the women from a fate worse than Kemp.'

Next day Klotz relieved me at the convent, for I still had work to do at Nakorn Panom. We had heard that there were some French families stranded at the Bartholony tin mines at Phon Tiou, twenty-five miles north of Thakhek, and so I've arranged that I should come back on the morrow, by which time Klotz hoped to have found a car to take us both to the mines.

When I returned on the morning of the 9th he had borrowed from the *Chaokhoueng* an old and dilapidated Citroën, whose engine popped and spluttered alarmingly as we drove through the neat, shady streets and out on to the laterite surface of the Route Coloniale 13. At first we followed the course of the Mekong, but after passing through Pak Hin Boun we turned due north and soon began to climb into the hills. The road ran through thick, overgrown forest, intersected by numerous tracks and varied occasionally by bright green patches of paddy or banana plantations; ahead the distant mountain tops shone blue and clear on the horizon, the patches of jungle on their slopes glowing emerald in the sunlight.

We met several convoys of lorries carrying armed Annamese to Thakhek. Each truck displayed a large red flag, and the young men riding behind gave us the clenched fist salute as we passed. Approaching the mines we were stopped several times by control posts, also decorated with the red flag and manned by youths in grey pith helmets; when I said I was a British officer they let us through without argument.

It was getting on in the afternoon when we reached the small cluster of bungalows that formed the living quarters of the mine officials. As we stepped out of the car a grey-haired Frenchwoman ran towards us gesticulating and sobbing piteously; her face was ravaged with lines of horror and despair. Taking us each by the arm she led us into one of the houses. Lying on a bed, wearing only a nightdress, was a girl of seventeen or eighteen; she was a very pretty girl, but now her face was sunken and waxy, her dark eyes hollow and lustreless.

'My daughter,' said the woman. 'Look!'

She lifted the girl's nightdress and pointed to the bluish puncture of a bullet wound about two inches below the navel. The girl looked at us without speaking, without interest. Her mother led us to another room, where lay a man of about fifty, a sallow death's-head who gazed at us in silence, but with tragedy and terror in his eyes.

'In God's name, madame,' said Klotz, 'what has happened?' Pulling herself together the woman told us the dreadful story.

She and her daughter had lived alone in this house since March, when the Japanese had taken her husband; the wounded man lived in the next bungalow with his wife. On 22nd August a party of Japanese, probably deserters, had burst in upon them, looted their houses and, in a fit of wanton cruelty, shot her daughter in the stomach with a pistol, put two bullets into their neighbour and murdered his wife.

'Obviously we must move them at once to Nakorn Panom,' said Klotz. 'But how can we take two badly wounded people, as well as this woman and ourselves, in our small Citroën? They won't survive the journey.'

'Let's try and borrow or hire something from the Annamese,' I suggested. 'Even a truck would do, and they seem to have plenty of those. I know they aren't friendly, but there must be somebody among them with a spark of humanity.'

I was wrong. We tried for an hour, approaching every lorry we saw and begging at least the kindness of a lift for one of the wounded and one of ourselves. At best we met indifference, at worst hostility.

'We can't leave them here, François,' I said. 'There's no alternative but to take a chance with the Citroën. Let's ask them how they feel about it.'

'But of course, gentlemen,' whispered the girl. She gave us a charming smile; only her eyes betrayed her fear.

'As for me,' murmured the man, 'I care nothing if only I can get out of here.'

They told us that there were some half-dozen more French civilians at the tin mines of Boneng, a few miles up the road. At the moment we could do nothing for them, but we resolved to come back with sufficient transport as soon as possible.

Gently we carried the girl into the car and placed her on the front seat; she made no complaint, despite her obvious suffering. Klotz took the wheel and the rest of us squeezed in behind. It was nearly dusk when we started; before we had covered five miles we were in darkness. The lights made a faint, ineffective glow.

'This battery is *kaput*,' Klotz called over his shoulder. 'I can hardly see the road, and if we run off it and have to stop we'll never get her started again. We must look for a village, or even a hut, where we can lie up for the night. In the morning we can find villagers who will push her until she starts.'

We drove at barely more than walking pace for another two miles until, across a paddy-field on the left of the road, we saw a light that seemed to indicate some dwelling.

'Keep the engine running, François, while I go and see if we can stay there.'

Although not usually a provident person I had remembered to bring a lamp. I made my way along a narrow path beside the field until I came to a small hut on the verge of the forest. A wiry, middle-aged Lao came down the steps carrying a torch of flaming brushwood. I pointed to the road and beckoned him to follow me, which he did without the least sign of surprise. When we reached the car he listened quietly while the wounded girl's mother, who spoke his language, explained our trouble. Then he smiled, and she translated his reply.

'He says we must stay with him for the night. He is a poor man and has little to offer us, but he will do his best to make us comfortable. There is a village four kilometres down the road to Thakhek. Tomorrow you can walk there and hire men to push the car.'

Very slowly, with the greatest care, we carried the girl along the path, the Lao preceding us with his torch; the wounded man followed, supported by the girl's mother. Even when we carried her up the steps of the hut the girl gave no sign of the pain she must have felt. There was only one room but it was spotlessly clean, as were the straw mats which were all our host could provide for bedding. I have seen many wounded in my life, and have been seriously wounded myself; but never have I met such fortitude, such indomitable spirit as that young French girl showed throughout her ghastly journey. Whenever either of us tried to sympathize or to apologize for her discomfort, she answered gently, 'It is nothing, monsieur,' and gave her soft, enchanting smile. The man, also, must have been in terrible pain; but he seemed too sunk in misery to care.

In the morning Klotz and I set off on foot down the road to get help, leaving the others in the care of the Lao. We found the village on a track about half a mile off the road. The headman, who spoke pidgin French, procured us the men we needed; but it took time to assemble them, for hurry is a word unknown in the Laotian vocabulary. Klotz decided to make his way separately to Thakhek, to send help to us in case we could not start the car.

He took a *pirogue* down the Nam Hin Boun, a small river which flows into the Mekong at Pak Hin Boun, and reached Nakorn Panom in the evening.

It was afternoon before we started the car and bowled down the road to Thakhek. Although light-headed from relief that our troubles were nearly over, as well as from lack of sleep, I took the journey very slowly, to avoid jolting the wounded. When we arrived at the quay I was thankful to find Smiley and Rowland Winn supervising the embarkation of the convent refugees and their very considerable quantity of luggage. Smiley had returned the previous night from Ubon with his order to Nakajima, and with a Japanese officer to see it carried out; on his instructions Nakajima's men had cleared the streets of Annamites who, despite their superior numbers, seemed to have a healthy respect for the Japanese. Winn had arrived from Naung Khai for a party which I had arranged but had forgotten in the emergency to cancel.

With the help of the Japanese, who carried the baggage, we finished the embarkation before dark; on the other side the Governor, Chief of Police and doctor were waiting with a large party of labourers, several lorries and a dozen bullock carts. Within two hours all the refugees were installed in the hospital, which the Governor had requisitioned for them; they were, naturally, almost hysterical with relief, and poured out their thanks to us all in such profusion that I thought we should never be allowed to leave.

The doctor examined the two wounded and made them as comfortable as possible; but he could not operate on them, lacking the instruments, anaesthetics and—by his own admission—confidence. We sent an urgent signal, asking for a Siamese Air Force plane to land on my airstrip and take them to Bangkok. The aircraft arrived ten days later; when I saw them again in Bangkok, in early November, they had both made a complete recovery.

Winn, too, had been busy at Naung Khai. At Vientiane the Franco-Laotian forces, under the veteran Commandant Fabre, were faced with stiff opposition, not so much from the Viet-minh, although they were active enough, as from the 'Free Lao' movement. This organization, in alliance with the Viet-minh, had declared an independent State of Laos, free from all French control, and had nominated a provisional government under the premier ship of Prince Phetsarath, a member of the royal house of Luang Prabang. Winn, who was working closely with Fabre, giving him what help he could, had to leave us next day to arrange the evacuation of French civilians from Vientiane.

The situation gave him scope for his impish and astringent wit. When Calcutta asked him for the names of the Provisional Free Lao Government he sent them the complete list, starting with Prince Phetsarath and ending with the words: 'But my favourite is Excellency Phoui repeat Phoui, Justice and the Arts.' Our staff officers in Calcutta were nearly always sympathetic and helpful; but on occasions they would send us the most senseless or irritating instructions. One of them, I remember, was to report on the number of elephants in our respective areas and their condition—some of the senior staff officers of Force 136 had interests in the Bombay-Burma Company; to this it was easy enough to reply that the only elephants we had seen were pink. But now, when they knew that we all had our hands full with the emergency in Indo-China, they chose to signal us:

'On leaving Field Finance Branch will require detailed accounts in ticals[1] and gold.'

---

[1] Siamese currency.

It was the timing we resented rather than the content. Winn drafted a bitter reply, concluding with the *cri-de-coeur*: 'Uncomplaining gravest difficulties here but how long oh how long must we continue to kick against the pricks in your office.'

It was late on that night of 10th September before we went to bed. We rose early to prepare for our journey to Boneng to rescue the remaining French civilians. Smiley, Klotz and I re-crossed the Mekong and went immediately to see Nakajima. That young officer was now only too anxious to help. At Smiley's request he provided us with a lorry and a Japanese escort with a light machine-gun, under the command of a lieutenant.

On the road we met few signs of life except an occasional water buffalo with a small boy perched upon its back, and a few peacocks which flitted across the road, gay and glorious in their bright plumage of blue and green. At the Bartholony mines we were stopped by some Annamese guards, who told us that there was a battle going on at Boneng between their troops and the French, and begged us to stop 'this French aggression against our people.'

As we approached Boneng we heard, above the noise of the engine, the sound of rifle and machine-gun fire. We left the lorry on the outskirts of the village and advanced through the town in battle order, the Japanese looking very grim behind their machine-gun, and the three of us doing our best to look resolute and undismayed.

The fighting was centred round the village school; there a small Franco-Laotian force was holding out against some hundred and fifty well-armed Annamites, who with four machine-guns were pouring an intensive if inaccurate fire into the wooden building. We approached the Viet-minh commander and Smiley ordered him to cease fire; after a moment's hesitation and a long look at our escort he obeyed. It now remained for us to parley with the French.

Telling Klotz and me to stay where we were and ignoring our anxiety for his safety, Smiley broke cover and walked boldly towards the school-house, waving a white handkerchief and calling out at intervals, '*Ne tirez pas, je suis officier anglais.*' With our hearts thumping we watched him walk slowly up the steps to the barricade across the door. He spoke for a few moments to someone inside, then beckoned to Klotz and me to join him.

We found a young French officer of Force 136, Lieutenant Gasset, a Eurasian sergeant and ten Lao soldiers. Gasset told us that he had entered the mines to rescue the French civilians there, but had been fired on by the Annamites, who had taken the civilians as hostages; he had evidently fought a good action, for his casualties were only two men wounded, whereas we saw, lying in the road outside, the dead bodies of four Annamites, and there were four more wounded.

Returning with Gasset to the Annamese lines we began to discuss with their commander some way of ending the conflict. During our talk the

Annamese insisted on producing for our close inspection the very messy bodies of their dead—as Smiley commented, they must have been unattractive enough when alive. Eventually we persuaded the Annamese to hand over their hostages and Gasset to return with his men to the mountains, leaving his two wounded Laos in our care.

The hostages were a man, four women and two children, all of them naturally very frightened. We lost no time in packing them and the two Laos into our lorry and driving away with our escort, happy in the fond belief that we had completed our work on that side of the Mekong.

III

MURDER ON THE MEKONG

Smiley returned to Ubon the next day to make arrangements for the transport of the prisoners of war to Bangkok and to disarm a Japanese division. Now that all the French civilians were safe we were ordered to interfere no more in Indo-China. I had, therefore, to leave Tavernier's problems to Klotz, who had already asked for a parachute drop of supplies and money for him.

Our refugees soon adapted themselves to their new life. In the single bare room that ran the whole length of the hospital they spread their mattresses and scanty possessions on the floor, grouping themselves by families in defiance of all the good Sisters' efforts to segregate the sexes. A few days of rest, decent food and, above all, freedom from fear, worked amazing changes in their appearance, especially among the women. After observing the effects of a little make-up and a lot of ingenuity on one or two of the girls, I began to regret that present circumstances did not allow me to cash in on my position as their liberator and protector.

The Siamese authorities did everything they could for them, and on 15th September we received our first drop—food, medical supplies and clothing. The refugees remained with us until the beginning of October, when all but the nuns and their orphan charges left for Ubon; there a French liaison officer met them and accompanied them to Bangkok. The nuns preferred to stay with us until conditions in Thakhek should permit them to return to their convent. An eighteen-year-old Eurasian girl, whom we called Jeannette, attached herself to my headquarters to help Rork and Edith Fournier with the very heavy cipher work, which was more than they could tackle by themselves. I had to ask permission from Calcutta to employ her, and somewhat to my surprise they agreed.

Pluto gave us a monkey, who lived on our veranda; he was very savage at first, having been badly teased by Pluto's young son, but Rork and I gradually tamed him, and he seemed to become very fond of us. He had some disgusting sexual habits which he usually indulged in the presence of young girls; Jeannette, who went about in shorts and bare legs, used to rouse him to a pitch of hysterical fury, and she could never go near him in safety. Later on we acquired from Indo-China two young male gibbons. They were enchanting creatures whose soft fur smelt deliciously of musk; they would cling to us, put their arms round our necks and pick imaginary parasites from our hair. One, whom we christened Toby, was black with a white face; the

34

other, who was white with a black face, we called Smift. The origin of his name needs some explanation. We frequently received signals ending with this obscure word; it was some time before we learned that it stood for 'See My Immediately Following Telegram'.

A few days after Smiley's departure a signal from Calcutta advised us of the decisions that had been taken at ' highest level' about the immediate future of Indo-China. South of the sixteenth parallel the country was in the S.E.A.C.[1] theatre of operations. As soon as their troops arrived, which would be in October, the French would take over the responsibilities of restoring law and order and disarming the Japanese; at present the only Allied military organization there was an Indian Division under General Gracey at Saigon. North of the sixteenth parallel, which included all the country adjoining our areas, those duties would be undertaken by Marshal Chiang-Kai-Shek's Kuomintang Chinese, whose troops were now advancing from the north and might be expected in Vientiane and Thakhek at any moment.

This news caused grave alarm among the Siamese, who had always feared—and still do—that their own large and unassimilated Chinese population might one day be used by China as a pretext for invading their country. Units of the Siamese Army and reinforcements of police began to move into our areas. The Governor looked worried and repeatedly stressed to me his anxiety. Although since the last century, when they had annexed Cambodia, the French had been the immediate object of Siamese fear and suspicion, always there had been the remoter but much more formidable menace of China.

In these new circumstances Force 136 lifted the ban on our intervention in affairs across the river, stipulating only that we should be accompanied wherever possible by French officers, and that we should tread very warily in our dealings with the Chinese; there was considerable danger, we were warned, of friction between the Chinese and the French. The British, on the other hand, were working very closely with the French, who needed our support badly in view of the American attitude to Indo-China. This signal concluded with a sentence so typical of the staff officer's mind that it is worth recording: 'You will give French all possible assistance short of becoming involved yourselves.'

The American attitude was summarized by the late Mr. Chester Wilmot, who wrote, 'Roosevelt was determined that Indo-China should not go back to France.' Mr. Graham Greene, who visited the country early in 1954, wrote of American intervention:

> In 1945, after the fall of Japan, they had done their best to eliminate French influence in Tongkin. M. Sainteny, the first post-

---

[1] South-East Asia Command, under Lord Mountbatten.

war Commissioner in Hanoi, has told the sad, ignoble story in his recent book, *Histoire d'une Paix Manqée*—aeroplanes forbidden to take off with their French passengers from China, couriers who never arrived, help withheld at moments of crisis.

We were shortly to witness even worse. Like ourselves the French had been accustomed to thinking of the Americans not only as allies but as friends; it never occurred to any of us simple officers that the most powerful country in the free world would deliberately embark upon a policy of weakening her allies to the sole advantage of her most dangerous enemy. We have learnt a lot since, but in those days it all seemed very strange.

Towards the end of the third week in September I paid Winn a visit at Naung Kai; Smiley had procured me from Bangkok a jeep, a three-ton lorry, two motor bicycles and several drums of petrol, so that communications were no longer a problem. The occasion for my journey was a party for Winn's twenty-ninth birthday, but its real object was to discuss in the light of our new instructions the problems facing us across the river.

Winn had evacuated from the other side a large party of French civilians, who were now under the care of the Governor of Naung Khai pending their departure to Bangkok; they were going by air, because the aerodrome at Naung Khai was large enough for Dakotas. Commandant Fabre's troops were in occupation of Vientiane, but they were not allowed to remain there long. At the end of the month the Chinese arrived in strength. Almost their first action was to invite all the French officers to a dinner-party. At the Chinese headquarters in the Residency, where the tricolour was flying in their honour, Fabre and his companions were courteously shown into a room and immediately surrounded by Chinese soldiers with levelled tommy-guns. They were relieved of their arms, equipment, money and watches and ordered to quit the town instantly, on pain of arrest. After some argument Fabre himself was allowed to stay, together with his wireless set and operator; but he had to send the rest of his force ten miles away, for he had been ordered to avoid incidents with the Chinese.

Defenceless and surrounded by enemies Fabre was vitally dependent upon help from Winn, who received parachute drops, including arms, and smuggled them across the river by night to a rendezvous with the Franco-Laotians in the jungle; more than once he had to smuggle not only arms but parachutists, for the French had no suitable dropping ground at their disposal. It was fortunate that the Governor of Naung Khai was sympathetic.

Winn's visits to confer with Fabre exposed him to grave personal risk. The distance from the landing-stage opposite Naung Kai to Vientiane was nearly fifteen miles—it was impracticable to make the journey direct by boat owing to the distance and the strength of the current; the Chinese had requisitioned all transport, and so Winn had to walk or bicycle. On the way he often found himself a target for Free Lao or Viet-minh snipers.

When, later on, he received a jeep his journeys became easier; but at the beginning of November he ran into an ambush and nearly lost his life. He was driving towards Vientiane with Fabre, a Lieutenant Larroue and two Lao soldiers when they were fired on at a range of fifty yards by about twenty Annamese with light machine-guns. He accelerated through the hail of bullets, but the jeep was hit, ran off the road and overturned; Winn broke a wrist, Fabre a shoulder and one of the Laos a leg. While the two uninjured men ran to get help Winn and his companions crouched for two hours in a ditch behind their vehicle, waiting for the enemy, whom they could plainly hear moving and talking in the undergrowth, to close in for the kill. But the enemy seemed to have no stomach for close fighting and kept their distance until a lorry arrived full of friendly Laos, who took the wounded men to safety.

A few days before my visit an American O.S.S mission of ten officers and N.C.O.s, under a Major Banks, had dropped without warning on the aerodrome at Naung Khai. Ignoring Winn they had established themselves in the town and prepared to receive supply drops. They had no authority from S.E.A.C. to be in Siam. Although perplexed and a little irritated by their discourtesy Winn was much more worried by their behaviour to Fabre and his officers, who at this time had not yet occupied Vientiane. From his base at Naung Khai Banks crossed the river on several occasions and in the most insulting manner ordered the French to keep out of the town and to 'cease their aggression' against the Annamese and Free Laos.

Determined to get rid of this nuisance Winn hit on the brilliant and comradely idea of persuading Banks that he would find a more interesting situation and greater scope for his activities at Thakhek.

'They left for Nakorn Panom yesterday,' he told me amiably when I arrived. 'You should find them there on your return.'

It is only fair to add that he would never have done it if he could have foreseen the consequences.

The birthday party took place in the Governor's house, where Winn had his headquarters; this was a tall white building over-looking the Naung Khai waterfront and the broad brown flood of the Mekong that swirled westwards from Vientiane in a great curve beneath the low red cliffs and bright green jungle of the Laotian bank. The Governor and his handsome wife, who had both taken a great liking to Winn and Lawson, had been at pains to provide the best food, unlimited liquor and the prettiest girls from the neighbourhood to make the party a success; Winn had also invited the French refugees from Vientiane. He had changed for the occasion into what my friend Hardy Amies might have called a daring and original number: a pair of black satin Chinese trousers, surmounted by a broad, multi-coloured silk cummerbund of Laotian design, an open-necked white silk shirt, and a green and white spotted silk scarf. I was unable to persuade him to wear his green forage cap as well. He had omitted to brush his hair but he smelt deliciously of Trumper's after-shaving lotion.

After the anxieties of the past weeks I was more than ready to enjoy myself; with the result that not all the events of that evening are clear in my memory. I have a blurred recollection of a totally uninhibited Spider Lawson causing some eyebrow-raising among those of the refugees who spoke English, with a spirited rendering of a famous soldiers' version of the Egyptian National Anthem; also of inflicting my attentions on a shapely and evidently nubile blonde, only to discover that she had formed an unshakable attachment to Lawson—'*Ce Spidair, donc,*' she kept whispering to me, '*croyez-vous que c'est un Homme Serieux?*'

Next morning we went to Vientiane for a meeting with H.H. Prince Phetsarath, self-styled Prime Minister of the Free Lao Government; he had promised to provide us with transport from the landing-stage, but for safety's sake we each took a pistol and an American .30 calibre carbine. Commandant Fabre met us at the landing-stage, a tall and silent man whose strong, determined features were drawn and sallow from months of malaria, dysentery and strain. A rickety old bus with a small escort of apathetic Chinese soldiers took us to Vientiane, a well-laid-out town of imposing white villas in spacious, shady gardens. In the largest, most luxurious, lived His Highness.

A swarthy, heavily built man in early middle age, he received us in a cool and comfortable room where the strong morning light filtered faintly through sun-blinds; his beautifully manicured hands and smart white linen suit matched the opulence of his surroundings. He had an unfortunate manner compounded of shiftiness, complacency and arrogance; nor were we impressed by his contemptuous references to our French friends or his exaggerated claims of the support he enjoyed among his people. But he mixed us a really excellent rum cocktail, which he described—with unconscious humour—as something between a *Cuba Libre* and a *Presidente*.

In the afternoon I drove back to Nakorn Panom full of anxiety about the O.S.S. mission Winn had wished on me. My fears were justified. Banks had set up his headquarters there, and had already received a drop on the airfield. He had also taken it upon himself to scare my French refugees out of their lives by telling them that they were going to be returned to Thakhek. But he was not seriously interested in Nakorn Panom, except as a base, and in me not interested at all. It was in Thakhek that he had made his presence felt. The Japanese had gone, leaving the town in the hands of the Viet-minh. In conferences with the Annamese Delegates, Banks assured them that he was determined to put an end to what he called French aggression; also that Chinese troops would shortly arrive to disarm the French and take over the administration of the country pending the establishment of a 'national and democratic government' in Indo-China, free from the rule of France.

In proof of his intentions he sought out Tavernier, whom he found holding a road block to the north of the town and brusquely ordered him to withdraw. To avoid incidents Tavernier complied, but afterwards he complained to me bitterly of Banks's tone and language.

'He spoke to me as I would not dream of speaking to a servant—in front of my own soldiers and the Annamites, all of whom understand French. He called me a pirate, and threatened that if I did not withdraw my men he would send Chinese troops to disarm us.'

By the same methods he had forced Quinquenel to abandon Savannakhet, which that officer had recently occupied.

The Annamese, of course, were delighted and immediately launched a series of sharp attacks on the French posts around both towns, forcing them to withdraw farther into the forest. I signalled Calcutta for instructions. They replied that Banks had no right to be in Siam, which came under S.E.A.C., we could not stop him making trouble in Thakhek, but he must do so from that side of the river. I should request him, tactfully, to remove his party. In the meantime Calcutta would take up the matter with S.E.A.C.

As diplomatically as I could I gave Banks the message. He was a spare, well-knit man in his early thirties, with a dark complexion, a thin, sneering mouth and flickering, close-set eyes; his manner was furtive and he seemed reluctant to look at me as he spoke. He told me curtly that he had his orders and meant to carry them out; he would stay at Nakorn Panom as long as it suited him and would make his own arrangements to receive drops on the airfield—he saw no need to give me warning of them.

I begged him to desist from encouraging the Annamese, who had been truculent enough before his arrival.

'After all,' I pointed out, 'the French are our allies. Tavernier and his men have held out with great endurance against the Japanese, to whom the Annamites gave their whole-hearted collaboration.'

'So did the French collaborate,' he snarled, his narrow eyes glancing around my feet. 'Why, I was betrayed myself by a traitor in France! It damn nearly cost me my life.'

Suppressing a wistful sigh I returned to my headquarters, where I drafted gloomy reports to Calcutta and Smiley.

Banks did in fact move within the next few days to Thakhek, where the Annamese were only too happy to find him a house. From time to time I received reports of his speeches, encouraging them in their 'struggle for freedom'. I must add that the others in his party were very different from their commander, being courteous, friendly and—on the few occasions when they were allowed—helpful; but they seemed overawed by Banks.

They had been gone two days when Klotz and I decided to visit Tavernier to hand over some medical stores; Klotz wrote to him to expect us. We should pass through Thakhek on the way, to pick up a car for part of the journey and carry out some commissions for the French. Banks had told Klotz to keep away, but he had replied with some heat:

'I can certainly go to Thakhek if I wish! I am a French officer and Thakhek belongs to France.'

We borrowed the Governor's launch with his two Annamese boatmen; the American Lieutenant Reese, who had come over that morning, was our only other companion. We started across the Mekong after lunch on 27th September. It is a date I am unlikely to forget. The monsoon was coming to an end; the afternoon was cloudless, still and warm; the hills behind Thakhek smiled peaceful and welcoming, a bright quilt of green and gold. The houses on the waterfront seemed deserted and asleep. We jumped ashore and walked up the ramp.

As we stepped on to the road we heard a high-pitched command, 'Halt!' From a doorway on the left issued a platoon of Annamese led by a short, lightly built officer with a drawn pistol, whom I recognized as one of the Viet-minh Delegates, known as Tu, formerly an employee of the electricity plant. In different circumstances he would have been a ludicrous figure with his dirty khaki shorts, the grey composition topee that seemed to be the uniform of his kind, and his self-important pseudo-military manner. He strutted up to us and made a signal to his men, who spread out facing us with levelled rifles.

'*Bien*,' he yapped, grinning to show a mouthful of uneven blackened teeth rotting in red, betel-stained gums. He turned to me. 'Who are you?'

'I am a British officer, as you know.'

'And you?' to Reese.

'American.'

'You,' he said to Klotz, 'are French?' Klotz nodded.

'Very well. The British and American officers may go free. They are our allies. The Frenchman is under arrest and will come with us. The French declared war on us yesterday in Saigon.'

'Don't be ridiculous,' I protested, trying to sound calm and confident. 'The British, Americans and French are all allies, and we are certainly not going to let you arrest our friend. Isn't that so, lieutenant?' I called to Reese, who had made his way through the rank of Annamese and was now leaning against the wall of a house across the road.

Reese shuffled his feet and looked unhappily at the ground. 'I don't know,' he muttered. 'I guess we're neutral.'

He looked miserable. I was and still am convinced that he was acting under orders; certainly he showed the next day that he had abundant moral courage, and I am certain that it was not physical cowardice that made him withhold his help from us at this moment.

I do not believe I have ever felt so utterly defeated. With Reese on one side of him and myself on the other it would have been possible to conduct Klotz back to the launch; I was sure the Annamese would not risk harming a British or American officer, and in this way we could have screened Klotz from their fire without much danger. Now I must try to do it alone, for it was unthinkable to leave him to certain murder and probable torture. What I would have given at that moment for just one section of British or Indian troops!

'François,' I said quietly in English, 'you and I are going back to the boat. There doesn't seem any future in staying here.'

He smiled and took his hand off his pistol holster. I turned to the Delegate, trying to keep my voice steady and conceal my fear.

'Monsieur Tu, since our presence here is unwelcome to you, my friend and I are returning to Siam. Au revoir.'

I made him a stiff bow and, putting my arm around Klotz and trying to keep myself between him and his enemies, turned and started to walk towards the ramp.

'No!' screamed Tu. 'You may go, but he stays here.'

'Keep moving,' I whispered, 'and pretend we haven't heard.'

Klotz nodded, his face expressionless, his eyes calm. I do not like to imagine his real feelings during those moments: I remember too vividly my own. But he gave no sign of the fear that must have been tormenting him; his frame beneath my arm was unshaking and relaxed. Behind us we heard the rattle of rifle bolts as the Annamese closed in. Please, dear God, I prayed, look after us now.

There was a shout from Tu, followed by a fusillade of shots about our ears. I felt the blast of a rifle on my right cheek and realized with a sudden surge of elation that they were firing past us or into the air. It was, after all, a bluff. Only a few yards ahead of us lay the launch under her dirty canvas awning; she was deserted, but if we could reach her safely and cast off from the bank, the current would take us downstream with enough steerage way to reach the Siamese side. I was now walking almost directly behind Klotz to give him the maximum of cover; it seemed that we had got away with it.

There was a fresh burst of firing; a figure ran up on my left, thrust his rifle under my arm into Klotz's back, fired once and disappeared. Klotz staggered and let out a terrible, despairing gasp.

'Oh, Peter,' he whispered. 'Oh, Peter!'

A wide crimson stain spread thickly over the front of his shirt; a torrent of blood poured from his mouth. I tried to hold him but he swayed forward out of my arms and lurched with weakening steps down the ramp on to the landing-stage; there he dropped on all fours and began to drag himself towards the launch. I ran after him and lifted him over the thwarts on to the raised after deck; he lay there face downwards, the blood trickling from his mouth. Within half a minute he was dead.

Nearly hysterical with anger and grief I ran back up the ramp. Tu and his men had vanished, but Reese was where I had left him, leaning against the wall; he had been joined by a major who was Banks's second-in-command and by two N.C.O.s.

'I hope,' I said, trying to keep my voice under control, 'I hope you're proud of your Annamite friends. 'That'—I pointed to the corpse on the launch—that is the direct result of your work!'

'Gee!" squealed a small dark boy, the younger of the N.C.O.s, 'Gee, this is terrible! Let's get the hell out of this place.'

'I guess,' said the major slowly, 'we better have a company of Chinese paratroopers down here right away. I'll go call Hanoi.'

Having failed to save Klotz's life I must at all costs rescue his body before the Viet-minh came to claim it as a token of their triumph. I was thankful to see the dowdy, sorrowful, figure of the *Chaokhoueng* approaching with the two Annamese boatmen who, not unnaturally, had run away when the trouble began. While they started the engine and swung the bows into the stream I sat down beside Klotz, brushing away the flies that were already clustered on his bloodstained mouth and back and on the congealing pool on the deck; they rose in a cloud with a low, resentful buzz.

All the way across I sat watching the poor dead face of this gallant, warm-hearted young man who in such a short time had become so close a friend. It seemed a tragic waste that after fighting throughout the war he should die now with a bullet in the back. I could not know how many thousands of his countrymen were to follow him in the next ten years. At that moment I felt only a bitter anger and a shattering sense of loss.

> So smothers in blood and burning
>   And flaming flight
> Of valour and truth returning
>   To dust and night.

Remorsefully I thought of how he had trusted my judgment when his own instinct had been to draw his pistol and stand his ground. If I had stood with him, threatening to shoot the first Annamese to lift a rifle, might he not, I now wondered, yet be alive? I am still haunted by the thought that it might have turned out better that way.

At Nakorn Panom I sent one of the boatmen with a note to the Governor, asking him to have the body delivered to the nuns, and to arrange a military funeral for the following afternoon; leaving the other man on guard at the wharf I walked to my headquarters.

Rork and Edith Fournier were on the veranda waiting for me; they had heard the shooting.

'Where is François?' Edith's voice was very low.

I could hardly bring myself to look at her: 'François is dead.'

She stood quite still and silent while the tears flooded into her eyes and fell in great glistening drops slowly down her cheeks. When I had told her what had happened she whispered, *'C'est la deuxième fois, mon Dieu, c'est la deuxième fois!'* On her last mission, in occupied France, her chief had been taken by the Gestapo. There was nothing I could say to her. Leaving her with Rork I shut myself in my room, fell upon the bed and for a few minutes gave in to my own misery and despair.

Pulling myself together I asked Edith to come with me to the hospital and break the news to the refugees and nuns before Klotz's body arrived. We covered the quarter of a mile distance without speaking. At the hospital we were surrounded by an anxious crowd, who stared in horror at my blood-stained clothes. When they heard that Klotz was dead there was a stunned silence, followed by a chorus of cries and sobs from the women; but their sorrow gave way to a rising clamour of indignation when I told them of Lieutenant Reese's neutrality.

While we were talking, the Governor arrived with the Chief of Police and the doctor. The doctor had already examined the body, which was now on the way to the hospital; he said that Klotz had been shot through the base of the heart and no power on earth could have saved him. The Governor was almost in tears himself with distress and anxiety. It appeared that the messenger to Tavernier had been intercepted by the Viet-minh, who had read Klotz's letter and prepared the ambush to meet us; by the time the Governor knew, Klotz had been killed. The order for Klotz's detention had been given by the Chief Delegate, Long, alias Le Hoq Minh, who had entrusted its execution to Tu. I asked the Governor to have them both arrested if ever they came to Nakorn Panom; but he could not do so without instructions from Bangkok, which despite my repeated efforts never arrived.

I gave him a telegram to send Smiley, asking him to come as soon as possible; with his rank and authority I felt that he might have some influence on Banks.

The nuns would lay out the body, and we would keep vigil over it in watches during the coming night. The funeral was arranged for the following afternoon, at the Catholic cemetery north of the town; the police would provide a guard of honour.

I spent the earlier part of the night drafting two long signals to Calcutta, one in clear giving them the facts, the other in code embodying my suggestions for bringing Klotz's murderers to justice and for helping Tavernier; I also wrote a detailed report on the incident and the events preceding it. The effort at least made me concentrate; I could not eat and it was useless to try and sleep.

At midnight we left for the hospital. I had ordered Rork not to stay long, for he had a heavy signal traffic in the morning; but Edith insisted on staying the rest of the night, and I could not prevent her. Klotz was lying on a camp bed, dressed in a clean uniform; he looked serene and peaceful, his strong features softened in the dim candlelight. We took our places among the shadowy figures thronging the small bare room. I found myself standing beside the Sheriff; all the officials of Nakorn Panom came to stand guard for a part of the night.

As the silent hours passed and I watched the calm, still face on the camp bed, I found I was no longer tortured by the terrible memory of that blood-drenched figure staggering down the ramp at Thakhek. Instead, I remembered François gently lifting in his strong arms the wounded girl at the mines; François reading me passages from Descartes and patiently and unsuccessfully trying to explain what Frenchmen meant when they described themselves as Cartésiens; both of us sitting over our rum on the veranda in the cool night, singing French Army marching songs. Into my mind came suddenly a verse from our favourite—sung, I believe, by the troops of General Juin in North Africa:

> *Il n'y aura plus de pierres,*
> *Il y aura des fleurs dans les jardins,*
> *Il y aura des oiseaux sur les branches légères*
> *—Il y aura des files sur tous les chemins.*

We were about to leave for the funeral when Lieutenant Reese arrived at the house, grim-faced but very smart in his uniform. He saluted me gravely.

'I've come, major, to attend Lieutenant Klotz's funeral.'

Edith turned and walked out of the room.

'That's very good of you, lieutenant, I'm sure. But—but—do you know what you may be letting yourself in for? The French here are pretty indignant and—'

'I know. But I'd like to be there.'

He walked with us to the cemetery. There he stood alone, his eyes on the ground, while the silent, fierce tide of hatred welled all round him. At last the priest began the service and everyone turned towards the open grave. When the coffin had been lowered, wrapped in the tricolour, the volley fired and the earth shovelled over, Reese turned to face the trench, saluted and marched away. Whatever may be said about him he showed that day no lack of dignity or courage.

The grave was marked with a plain wooden cross inscribed with Klotz's name and the date of his murder. It was not allowed to remain there long.

The Annamese, whose town adjoined the cemetery, could not let their hatred rest with his death; time and again during the next three months they uprooted the cross and took it away, leaving a few splinters to mock his trampled grave. Each time we replaced it they would do the same: an easy revenge, but what a people that could find it sweet.'

When we had thanked the Governor and all his officers, Edith, Rork and I walked slowly homewards along the road by the Mekong bank. Gazing at those hateful hills above Thakhek which only yesterday I had thought so beautiful, I felt Edith's tight grip on my arm. 'Nous le vengerons,' she whispered fiercely, '*nous le vengerons!*'

Before we reached the main street we met Smiley, driving a large Cadillac saloon which he had taken from a Japanese general. My telegram had found him at Mukdahan, where he had gone to take over the Japanese ships on the Mekong; he had driven here at full speed.

When he had heard my story he wrote a note to Banks asking for an interview in Thakhek the next morning and for an escort to take him from the boat to O.S.S. headquarters. He ordered me to stay behind, and in the circumstances I could not argue. But I tried to stop him going alone, because I had heard that the Viet-minh had announced that any officers, of whatever nationality, who had been helping the French would be arrested if they came to Thakhek.

I was very glad to see him back in the afternoon.

'What did you think of Banks?' I asked.

Smiley made a rude gesture. 'Apart from everything else, he can't tell the truth. He swore to me that he had never called the French officers bandits or ordered them to give themselves up to the Annamese; but he didn't know that I had in my pocket a letter written by him to the French at Savannakhet in those very words. By the way, Peter, you're not to go to Thakhek again. The Viet-minh are after your blood and they've put a price on your head.'

'How much?'

'I can't quite make out. It's either five hundred pounds or half a crown, depending on the rate of exchange.'

IV

PERILS OF A GUN-RUNNER

At the beginning of October I had news from Calcutta that S.E.A.C. were pressing for the withdrawal of Banks and his party. I was ordered to tell him that the Viet-minh had just shot up O.S.S. headquarters in Saigon and killed Colonel Dewey, the Commander.

To my surprise the news made no impression on him, he had already heard it. He simply repeated that he had his orders. However, at the end of the week his entire party left for Ubon; I never saw them again. At this point I must make it clear that Major Banks was quite unlike any other American officer I have ever met; moreover, the other members of his mission seemed a friendly and well-intentioned body of men. If I have been unable to hide my bitterness against Banks it is because he was largely responsible for the murder of my friend and for the strengthening of Viet-minh resistance around Thakhek which was to cause the French so many casualties in the next six months. What I cannot explain is how he was able to use Siamese territory as a base in contravention of a clear agreement between the British and United States governments.

That Smiley had been right about the Viet-minh attitude towards me was soon apparent. Interested in locating their positions facing Tavernier south of the town, I borrowed the Governor's launch one afternoon and cruised up and down close to the other bank of the river, studying the shore through my field glasses. This pleasant pastime came to an abrupt end when, without warning, several machine-guns opened up on us, fortunately firing short. Sang-a, the only other passenger, threw himself on the floor—wisely—and lay there gibbering. I did not have to tell the helmsman to turn away; before I could give the order he had the launch headed at full speed for home. I reflected that if it were true, as we had heard, that the Viet-minh had Japanese deserters in their ranks, it was lucky for us that none of them was behind those guns.

On various occasions during the next four months I and the officers attached to me were sniped on the road; but the Annamese were not sure enough of themselves to pursue their vengeance very vigorously in Siam— or so, at least, I thought.

One of the suggestions I had made in my signal on the night of Klotz's death was that supplies of arms should be dropped to me to smuggle to Tavernier; two days later Calcutta agreed, and told me to stand by for a drop on 3rd October; I had also asked to receive French parachutists, as Winn had been doing at Naung Khai, and transport them across; but this was not agreed until some weeks later. I was particularly warned not to divulge the fact that I was smuggling arms; I was to pretend that the containers held medicines, food and clothing—as indeed a few of them would. I decided to visit Tavernier immediately to plan our gun-running operation.

Tavernier's headquarters was still at Ban Tung. I asked him to have men and horses waiting for me at a small village on the far bank of the Mekong, about ten miles south of Thakhek. On 1st October I borrowed the Governor's launch and crossed over in the morning. Tavernier's men were waiting—six young Lao soldiers under a French N.C.O.

We rode along narrow winding tracks through thick undergrowth, frequently having to lean over our ponies' necks to avoid branches and creepers that overhung our path. After half an hour we began to climb gradually into the hills. We had covered about ten miles and climbed a thousand feet when we came suddenly upon the familiar banana plantations that marked the outskirts of a village; here we were challenged by an outpost of three Lao soldiers with an old Hotchkiss light machine-gun. A few minutes later we came into a wide clearing dotted with huts and a few small houses, which was the village of Ban Tung. Laotian soldiers—barefooted little men in shorts and dark blue berets—walked between the huts in twos and threes, or squatted in groups in the doorways, chatting and laughing; all had the same alert, expectant look. Dismounting, I followed the N.C.O. to the largest of the houses, which was Tavernier's command post, and waited on the veranda while he announced me with an impressively smart salute.

Lieutenant Ferdinand Tavernier was a tall, dark officer of about my own age; lean and ascetic in appearance, prematurely bald, with tired eyes blinking behind thick horn-rimmed glasses, he seemed a good deal older. He spoke in a quiet, rather high voice and he very seldom smiled; he had no English.

I had brought with me a few medical stores and told him that there were more waiting for him at Nakorn Panom. He was pathetically grateful.

'You know, major, there is not one of us here who is not sick. All of us have recurring malaria, most have amoebic dysentery, and our small stock of medicines was long ago exhausted. We have had no supplies since the Japanese coup in March.'

Making a note of his most urgent needs I asked, 'Have you had any cases of bacillary dysentery?'

'Oh yes, plenty. But they all died.'

We arranged that he should come to Nakorn Panom the day after the drop; we would load his stores on to one of my lorries and drive to a point about fifteen miles south of the town, where he would have men and *pirogues* waiting to transport them over the river.

'This is wonderful news!' he exclaimed. 'We are really desperate here. Since our Major Banks gave them such encouragement the Annamites have been pressing us hard; with the few weapons I have I cannot stand up to them, and now I am running out of ammunition. I could, of course, retire deep into the mountains, but that would mean leaving the population here, who are our friends, to be massacred.

'Do you think you could also get me some money to buy food? We cannot continue to live indefinitely on the charity of these good people. And of course my soldiers have not been paid since March. It is wonderful the way they have stood by us, when they could so easily have deserted.'

There was no other officer with Tavernier, but I was introduced to his N.C.O.s. Sickness, undernourishment and fatigue made them look like walking corpses, but they were all cheerful and full of hope and enthusiasm. The most impressive figure was the padre, a short, square Frenchman with a huge black beard, a deep voice and an apparently inexhaustible fund of energy and good humour.

On the way back to the launch I was riding at the head of the party; as I leaned forward to pass under an overhanging branch I heard a sharp cry from the man behind '*Attention, Commandant!*' Looking back I saw, coiled along the branch I had just passed, a large snake. That was the only live snake I saw in the Far East, outside the pits of the Pasteur Institute in Bangkok.

My carefully disseminated cover-story about the arms was shattered during the drop by one of those pieces of bad luck which always seem to catch me out when I embark upon deception. The two Liberators made their dropping runs from west to east, turning at the end of each run when they were over Thakhek. Owing to a fault in the release mechanism one of the containers stuck underneath the aircraft, falling a few seconds later on the far bank; it was retrieved by the Viet-minh, who thus received a present of eighteen Stens, as well as valuable material for propaganda, of which they made immediate use.

The next morning the Governor came to see me in a state of extreme indignation, forbade me to move the arms I had just received, and placed a police guard over them. Even Smiley was unable to mollify him; the most he would allow poor Tavernier to take were the containers that actually held only food, clothing and medicine, and the money which I had received on his behalf.

I sent an urgent signal to Calcutta, asking for instructions to be sent from Bangkok for the release of the arms; but it was a fortnight before they arrived. Even then the Governor insisted that the operation should be carried out at night, and well away from the town. I therefore wrote to Tavernier asking him to send *pirogues* and men to a small village on the Siamese bank of the river, a little way upstream of our original rendezvous; they were to await me there at midnight on 20th October. I decided to accompany the arms across the river and see them delivered personally—partly to satisfy myself about their condition, and partly because it would give me the opportunity of having a further talk with Tavernier and assessing his future requirements.

I could scarcely hope for complete secrecy in smuggling the arms, after the publicity that had attended their arrival; the Governor, however, tactfully removed our police guards at dusk on the 20th, and so gave us the chance to load the containers on to our lorry under cover of darkness. It was a slow and exhausting business but, exhilarated by the thought that we were doing something, however small, to avenge poor Klotz, we quite literally put our backs into the work.

Leaving Edith Fournier behind to operate the wireless sked Rork and I set out for the rendezvous shortly after eleven, with Rork at the wheel.

'I hope to God the French are there on time,' I commented as we bumped over the pot-holes on the road leading southwards from the town and left the last huts and plantations behind. 'I shan't feel happy so long as this stuff remains on Siamese soil. Those Annamite bastards must have a pretty good idea of our plan, and I wouldn't put it past them to try and intercept—in which case I don't at all care for the thought of waiting around on our own in the dark in the middle of the countryside.' 'No more do I, sir. D'you really think they'll try something here? I don't think the Governor would like that much.'

'No, he certainly wouldn't. But I don't want to take chances, just the same. Of course, they may try to catch us on the river—they ought to be able to see all right with this moon. 'That reminds me,' I went on. 'In my letter, I gave Tavernier to understand that I should be returning tomorrow by the same route, and you'd be picking me up in the truck at this same village. Now of course that would be a dotty idea. If the Annamese are really out to get us, it's the obvious place they'd choose to lie in wait.'

'But how will you really get back?'

'Quite simply. Before we left home tonight I wrote a line to the Governor—I have it on me now—asking him to send his launch tomorrow morning to collect me from the other side and take me direct to Nakorn Panom. You will please deliver it to him personally first thing in the morning.'

'I will, sir. But will he agree?'

'Certainly, he'll agree. I've explained that I'm afraid of trouble from Comrade Tu and his pals, and that's something he's as keen to avoid as we are.'

We drove on in silence until we came to the track leading to the village where I was to meet Tavernier's men; it ran off to the left, just before the road crossed a narrow wooden bridge over a watercourse. Rork slowed down.

'Better turn her round,' I said, 'so that we're facing homewards in case of trouble.'

'We're a bit late for that, sir. Look!'

In the moonlight I saw two figures standing by the posts on either side of the bridge; at the same moment two more appeared from the bushes at the entrance to the track. I fumbled for my pistol and was about to shout to Rork to put his foot on the accelerator when, with an almost sickening flood of relief, I noticed the berets and uniform shirts of Tavernier's Laotians.

There were more than a dozen men awaiting us, not all of them soldiers; in command was one of the N.C.O.s I had met on my first visit. Under his direction they set to work swiftly and quietly, opening the containers and carrying the weapons and boxes of ammunition down the few hundred yards of track to the river. When the last empty container had been replaced in the lorry I gave Rork my note to the Governor.

'Mind you hand it to him personally,' I repeated.

'I will, sir, never fear. Good luck to you now.'

He drove off into the night. Slinging my carbine on my shoulder I followed on the heels of the French sergeant, picking out the pale ribbon of the winding path between dark clumps of thorn bushes. Once or twice I stopped and looked around uneasily, to reassure myself that we were not being followed; but the fields lay still and peaceful in the milky moonlight. We slowed our pace when we entered the coconut plantations on the outskirts of the village, making a wide detour to avoid the houses. A gentle breeze rattled the palm fronds overhead and brought to our nostrils the heady, sweet scents of the tropical night mingled with the reek of wood smoke from dying fires; from close by came the snarling bark of a dog, followed by a brief chorus of yelps that gradually died away into silence.

Six or seven large *pirogues* were lying at the water's edge. The work of loading was completed with the same speed and silence as before. There was no sign of life from the village as we climbed aboard and paddled away from the bank; even the dogs had ceased their howling, and the only sounds in the still night were the gentle splash of our paddles, the gurgle of water against the hulls and the faint whispers of the Laotian crews.

Reclining in the centre of my canoe on top of some salvaged parachutes and propping my back none too comfortably against a small pile of ammunition boxes in the stern, I gazed at the stars and abandoned myself to some sardonic reflections on the many unmilitary disguises I had been called upon to assume during my employment with S.O.E. In my time I had played the part of a journalist, a commercial traveller, a diplomat, a politician, a brigand, and even a gigolo—I did not care to dwell on that desperate occasion in a neutral country when a cynical superior had ordered me, in the interests of the King's Service, to seduce a lady suspected of dealings with the enemy: an experience so shattering that I still sweat with embarrassment at the memory. Recently I had been a sort of District Commissioner, and now I was a smuggler. This last, at least, was respectable; moreover, the operation had gone without a hitch. It seemed too good to be true: indeed it was.

For the first part of the journey we set a course slightly upstream, to take advantage of the current later on. From my position, roughly in the middle of the flotilla, I kept an anxious watch for our enemies, but the only signs of human life other than ourselves were an occasional *pirogue*, obviously engaged in fishing, and one or two lights on the farther bank—probably the fires of charcoal burners; the only movement that caught my eye was the shimmer of the moon on the swiftly gliding water and the dancing points of light where the river raced over the shoals among the blue and silver shadows of the sandbanks.

In the middle of the river, a little more than half-way across, lay a small island, a long, low strip of jungle whose tree-fringed shore showed dark against the distant background of the Cammon hills. As we approached it we began to alter course to pass below its southern tip.

'Who lives there?' I asked the French sergeant, who was sitting immediately in front of me.

'Oh, nobody. The fishermen use it sometimes, and we too, when we cross the river, halt there to rest ourselves a while. But tonight,' he flashed me a smile over his shoulder, 'with this valuable cargo perhaps we had better hurry on our way.' I was to thank my guardian angel for the haste.

As I watched the trees glide past I strained my eyes to peer into the gloom of the undergrowth, wondering if any hidden enemies were lying in wait for us; but I could see no movement in that strip of silent jungle. I lay back with a sigh, and marvelled again at the moonlit beauty of this mighty and mysterious river which ran for nearly three thousand miles from the Tibetan Plateau to the South China Sea. What a romantic setting, I gloated, for a smuggler!

We were rounding the tip of the island, less than two hundred yards from the shore, when an abrupt challenge rang out from the darkness, shattering my reverie; I clutched at my carbine as a burst of machine-gun fire ripped up the water a few yards away. A second burst slammed into the leading canoe, toppling the bow paddler straight over the side; the steersman slumped slowly forward and sideways and, as he fell, the canoe heeled over and capsized with a great splash and flurry of foam. The third occupant appeared for a moment in the water, grabbing frantically at the slippery bottom of the dug-out as it spun away on the current; but he stood no chance, and in a few seconds was swept from our sight with a sickening cry of terror and despair.

The sergeant bellowed an order in Lao, and our *pirogue* swung sharply downstream, almost tipping me overboard as the crew drove their paddlers into the water to speed us away from that murderous and cunning trap. The little island, which had seemed a moment earlier so quiet and aloof, was now erupting with the ragged crackle of rifle-fire and the vicious stammer of the machine-gun; the sound of the fusillades rolled across the river to echo back to us from the distant hills.

I imagine that a smuggler can have few more disagreeable experiences than that of coming under heavy fire at close range in a flimsy canoe on a fast and turbulent river. As the bullets smacked into the water around us, or zipped frighteningly past my ears, or whined in angry richochet among our scattering flotilla I let go of my carbine and lay back as far as I could, gripping the gunwales tightly to brace myself against every lurch and twist of our plunging craft. I was acutely conscious, also, of my proximity to the ammunition cases, and wondered unhappily whether it would be more uncomfortable to be blown to glory or downed in the Mekong. Were there crocodiles in the Mekong, I asked myself; I had heard there were some in the tributaries. And hippopotami? No, you bloody fool, they're in Africa. But there may be crocs; they'll be lying on the sandbanks disguising themselves as logs of wood. I began to giggle foolishly until I saw the sergeant give me a worried glance.

Thoroughly ashamed, I picked up my carbine and, wriggling over on to my stomach facing the stern, began to shoot back at the island. There was not the least likelihood, of course, of my hitting anybody—except perhaps the paddler in the stern, whose nervousness increased noticeably with each shot I fired—but I thought it showed the right spirit, and at least it made me feel better. It was obviously having the opposite effect on the poor paddler, who, with bullets flying past him from both directions, was rapidly approaching hysteria; moreover, my efforts were endangering the balance of the boat. I rolled over again on to my back and tried to lie still, praying feverishly that we should soon be out of effective range.

Fortunately the enemy's fire, after that early unlucky burst, was not very accurate. Untrained troops, as the Annamese were, tend to fire high, especially at night: fortunately, also, they seemed to have only one machine-gun, and they had no tracer to help them correct their aim. They had probably hoped to take us by surprise on the island. Clearly visible as we had been at first in the moonlight, now that we had scattered we presented more difficult targets; moreover, the strong current, combined with the efforts of the paddlers, was rapidly increasing the range. Their shots went wider with each minute of our flight, and soon they ceased to trouble us, although they continued to blaze away sporadically in our direction almost until we landed.

It was indeed a miraculous escape, and I poured out my thanks to providence for the sergeant's decision not to stop for a rest on that island. In the capsized canoe we had lost two Lao villagers and one soldier, as well as a number of Stens and some food and clothing; otherwise our only casualties were two men slightly wounded, both of them able to walk.

As I checked the stores next morning with Tavernier, he said to me: 'In future I think it is better if we use no couriers but mine to carry letters concerning the delivery of arms. The Annamites will always try to intercept our correspondence, and in Lakhon you do not know who you can trust. But

I can always send men of proved fidelity. So next time you have some material for me, send me word and I will send you a courier to whom you can entrust the details of a rendezvous. It will take a little longer, but it will be much safer.' I could only agree.

As had expected, the Governor's launch arrived to take me back, and a very worried Governor came to meet me at the landing-stage at Nakorn Panom. I tried to make light of the incident, although I knew he would learn the full story soon enough. But when I reached home Edith Fournier was looking 'very grave.

'I hear you had trouble on the river, Peter.'

'Yes, a little. There was some treachery, I'm afraid.'

'There was indeed. It is as well you did not come back the same way this morning. The *curé* of the church by the *ville annamite* was here. Although he is an Annamite himself he is a good friend of ours, and he hears a lot of things. He was very worried because the Annamites had arranged another little reception for you at that village where you and Rork went last night.'

A few days later I received an enthusiastic letter of thanks from Tavernier. The Viet-minh had launched a heavy attack on Ban Tung the night after I had left. Thanks to the arms, and more particularly the ammunition, I had brought him he had been able to hold his ground; but for their timely arrival lack of ammunition would have forced him to withdraw. In the following weeks I took him several more consignments; some of the arms I received by parachute drop, others came from Smiley, who was able to draw on Japanese dumps. Each time we varied our rendezvous, using Tavernier's couriers as we had arranged; there were no more incidents.

I celebrated my reconciliation with the Governor by inviting him to a dinner party; I thought it an appropriate occasion to ask also the Chinese colonel at Thakhek and his staff. From the colonel I received a most courteous letter thanking me in flowery language for my invitation and ending sadly with the words, 'We are sorry we cannot come because we have a sore foot.'

During this time I made one visit to Savannakhet, by night, for a clandestine meeting with Quinquenel to discuss arms deliveries. Crossing the Mekong by *pirogue* I was met at the landing-stage by two Laos soldiers, who led me through silent and empty streets, flooded in moonlight, to a large house at the back of the town. I knew that Quinquenel had evacuated Savannakhet, but it seemed that the Viet-minh had not been able—or had not bothered—to occupy it themselves. However, we were taking no chances, and padded swiftly and noiselessly through the streets, keeping, wherever possible, to the shadows.

Awaiting me with Quinquenel was a thick-set, broad-shouldered Laotian who was later to exercise a profound influence on the history of his country.

Chao (Prince) Boun Oum of the royal house of Champassak—the old southern Laotian kingdom suppressed by the French—had the intellectual outlook of a European superimposed on the instincts of a Laotian patriot.[1] A passionate Francophile who had received his education in France, he had played a leading part in the resistance against the Japanese. Now he was preparing to throw the full weight of his very considerable influence in this area behind the French and against the Viet-minh.

Thereafter, as long as I remained on the frontier, a large part of my time was spent in running arms to the French—both to Tavernier and to Quinquenel, with whom I arranged a secluded rendezvous on the river south of Mukdahan. These officers needed everything we could send them; they were continually engaged in savage battles against superior forces, and their own Command in Saigon was in no position to help. But on 19th October they received their first reinforcements: sixty-four French parachutists dropped on my airfield and, after an enormous lunch which Tavernier attended, were ferried across the river in *pirogues*. By the time our missions left the area, at the end of January 1946, the French were able to take the offensive; two months later they were in possession of Thakhek and Savannakhet.

Apart from gun-running my principal duty was the filing of intelligence reports, known as 'sitreps', to Calcutta and later to the G.O.C. in Bangkok, General Evans. There was, in fact, much more work than I could tackle alone; and so I was delighted when, towards the end of October, two officers arrived to help me. They were Major Cox and Captain Maynard, and they brought with them a wireless operator, Corporal Powling. They installed themselves at Mukdahan.

Cox was a clever and experienced officer who had served with Force 136 in Burma; his gift for extracting the maximum amount of quiet fun out of life made him a delightful companion. Maynard was a young man of twenty-two whose ingenuity and enthusiasm more than compensated for any lack of maturity. Powling, a tall, quiet, very young soldier, most efficient at his job, unfortunately died the following January from virulent smallpox.

One of Maynard's first actions was to design and build a motor *pirogue* to help us with our gun-running. He recruited a squad of skilled Siamese workmen and a competent mechanic, and bought from a Chinese merchant an outboard motor in excellent condition. In a remarkably short space of time we had a stout and swift little craft, fitted with a half-deck forr'd; in the bows we mounted a Bren gun. We now felt able to deal with any attempt by the Annamese to interrupt our convoys on the water. In deference to the Viet-minh's Radio Hanoi, which had been denouncing us a 'brigands and pirates', we persuaded the nuns to embroider us a silken ensign with a skull

---

[1] He is, at the moment of writing, Prime Minister of Laos.

and crossbones, which streamed proudly in the breeze above the puttering outboard motor. We had to be careful, however, because the very sight of our toy gunboat would rouse the Annamese machine-guns to a fury of activity; they would open fire on us even when we were cruising close in to the Siamese shore.

On 26th October a medical officer was attached to my headquarters. Captain Donald Gunn, R.A.M.C. was quiet, most conscientious and extremely efficient, he was about twenty-six and had previously worked behind the Japanese lines in Burma. His confident, unruffled manner, dry sense of humour and abundant common sense vastly increased his value to our party. Sickness and enemy action took a constant toll of the French forces; to Nakorn Panom, Mukdahan and Naung Kai they brought their casualties for treatment and evacuation by air to Bangkok. Gunn's life was an exacting round of journeys between the three stations; after driving all night to attend a batch of wounded he would often have to drive back sleepless through the following night for further work elsewhere. In the intervals he found time to help us with the problems of administration and the reception and disposal of parachute stores; he did not seem to need rest.

Smiley had cultivated excellent relations with the Siamese Air Force, especially with the station commander at Korat, Wing-Commander Manop Souriya, who was known even to his brother-officers as Nobby; the Wing-Commander, who had passed through West Point and served an attachment to the R.A.F. before the war, proved himself a firm and valuable friend. Aware of our difficulties with communications, he obtained permission from his superiors to send an aircraft and pilot to Ubon for Smiley's personal use. The aircraft was a dual-control Mitsubishi Advanced Trainer, an obsolete monoplane of doubtful reliability, with seating for one passenger in comfort and a precarious perch for a second in the tail; it did not prove as useful as we had hoped, because it spent most of the time on the airfield at Ubon or Korat undergoing repairs or awaiting spare parts. We were none too happy to learn that the pilot's name was Pilot Officer Prang.

My first flight in the machine was on 31st October, when Smiley and I were summoned to Bangkok, he for a conference with General Evans and Brigadier Jaques, I for my first meeting with the Brigadier. We took off from Nakorn Panom after breakfast, with Smiley sitting behind the pilot, and myself squatting on a discarded parachute, a prey to acute discomfort and claustrophobia. Our first call was at Udaun, thirty-five miles south of Naung Kai, where we had an appointment with Winn. We reached it in an hour, flying at a thousand feet and following the narrow pink strip of laterite road that ran almost straight through the feathery carpet of forest.

Planning to lunch at Korat, nearly two hundred miles to the south, we left Udaun at noon and climbed to five thousand feet, to cross a high range of mountains. After an hour's flying we saw them beneath us—jagged outcrops of rock thrusting malevolently up towards us through the bright green profusion of hostile jungle; deep-shadowed gorges twisting sharply between the peaks. If the engine fails now, I thought, we haven't a hope of making a landing.

Of course it did fail, in a series of sharp, angry backfires while Prang fiddled furiously with various switches on the instrument panel; then it cut and left us gliding through the air in a grim and fearful silence. Smiley turned round in his seat to catch my eye, the corners of his mouth twisted comically downwards as he pointed to the savage mountains below. R.A.F. pilots had told me that if your engine failed while flying over jungle, and there was no paddy in sight, the best chance was to land on top of bamboo.

'Do you see any bamboo down there?' I asked. Smiley shook his head, obviously thinking that terror had deprived me of my wits.

At that moment the engine spluttered into life and we breathed again. But not for long. Five times in the next half-hour this terrifying performance was repeated, while we steadily lost height, until, at two hundred feet above the ground, clear at last of the mountains, we saw ahead of us the comforting expanse of Korat aerodrome. There was no safety margin for a circuit, and so we came straight in, landing with the wind in a frightening succession of vicious bumps, breaking off a wheel and slewing sideways on the starboard wing in a cloud of choking red dust. Leaping from the aircraft Smiley and I stood shaking and sweating on the runway while Prang climbed slowly down and gazed at us in silence with a bashful, apologetic and wholly disarming smile.

Strong drinks and lunch with Nobby restored our nerve sufficiently to fly on with Prang in another aircraft. We reached Bangkok in the last daylight and in time for a spectacular party given by Force 136 in the palace of one of the royal princes. I had never thought our frontier life uncomfortable, but I was staggered by this sudden projection into luxury, and felt awkward and scruffy in my faded battledress beside the trim little Siamese officers and the British in their well-tailored uniforms. The women dancing under the coloured Chinese lanterns or gliding across the lawns in the clear, warm, scented moonlight seemed each one an Aphrodite of voluptuous grace and sensuality. Sadly I noted that none of them showed the least interest in me.

The following day passed in an endless succession of conferences. Force 136 was going into liquidation but a few of our missions in Siam, including those on the north-east frontier, were being retained in a new organization, Allied Land Forces Paramilitary Operations, under the direct orders of the G.O.C., General Evans. Smiley and Winn were returning to England at the end of November, the former to attend his Staff College course, the latter for demobilization. I was asked to take over Smiley's command, an offer which delighted me; I should be the only remaining officer with experience of the north-eastern frontier and, having no urgent reason to return home, I felt that I must stay to give all possible help to our Franco-Laotian Allies who had so deeply inspired me by their devotion and courage.

We left Bangkok after lunch on 2nd November and landed at Korat without incident; when we took off again Smiley, who had flown his own aircraft before the war, was at the controls. We were gaining height over the aerodrome when there was a violent jar on the port wing; as the aircraft shuddered and banked at a dangerous angle I peered over the cockpit, to see a long, deep gash in the leading edge, about half-way along. Smiley quickly adjusted the trim and returned to land safely. It turned out that we had collided with a very large bird, which fortunately had struck the wing and not the propeller; but the dented metal had jammed the connecting wires to the ailerons and we were lucky to have avoided a crash.

After a half-hour's delay we left in the machine which had brought us to Korat two days before. By now we were both thoroughly apprehensive of Siamese aircraft, or at least of Advanced Trainers, and we only began to breathe freely when we saw to starboard the hill above Sakon Nakorn, a round furry pimple in the forested plain, and flew over the reed-fringed lake where in August I had tried to shoot duck. The mountains of Laos loomed closer through the haze, and I sighed contentedly when I caught sight of the houses of Nakorn Panom straggling down towards the mudbanks exposed by the subsiding waters of the Mekong. I was not even alarmed when, as we swung in to land, the engine spluttered once or twice and cut. We glided in and bumped gently over the landing-strip to a halt.

'What was the cause of that?' I asked Smiley a little later.

'Oh, it seems they forgot to fill her up at Korat. She was clean out of gas when the engine cut. Aren't we the lucky ones?'

I had a better chance of seeing Bangkok in the middle of November, when I was summoned there for a detailed briefing by the G.O.C. on the duties of my new command. We flew no more in Siamese aircraft, but depended for our air communications on a flight of R.A.F. L5s based on the racecourse on the outskirts of the capital.

Brigadier Jaques had already gone, although Smiley and Winn were in Bangkok awaiting transport home. The new office of ALFPMO was controlled by two majors, Tom Hobbs and David Muirhead; they were able and conscientious officers, grossly overworked and understaffed, but with their anxiety to help and their rare skill at extracting precious stores from the harassed Q branch, they were to prove invaluable allies during the ensuing two months. From them I graduated through the offices of the GI Operations and the GI Intelligence to the presence of my new master, Major-General Geoffrey Evans, commanding 7th Indian Division and British Troops Siam.

Robustness, which Lord Wavell considered the most important quality in a modern commander, was evident both in General Evans's military record and in his personal appearance. As a brigade major in 4th Indian Division he had served in the first Western Desert campaign in 1940 and afterwards at the storming of the Keren heights in Eritrea—the most arduous battle, he told me, he had ever fought. As a brigadier in 5th Indian Division he had commanded the Sinzewia box in the bitter Arakan fighting of 1944, when 5th and 7th Indian Divisions were surrounded and narrowly escaped annihilation. After commanding a brigade at the siege of Imphal he had become G.O.C. successively of 5th and 7th Indian Divisions. A short, solidly built man in his middle forties with close-cropped greying hair and moustache, firm features in a rounded face and a determined thrust to his jaw, he combined with a gruff, sometimes abrupt, manner of speech, a cool, alert mind, a shrewd judgment and a dry, ironic wit. With none of the suspicion and dislike of paramilitary operations sometimes found in regular soldiers he showed a clear understanding of the situation on the frontier and of our difficulties in meeting it; and he promised me his full support in our efforts—a promise which he fulfilled beyond all my hopes.

Our principal task, he explained, would be the gathering and grading of intelligence, especially political intelligence; we must pay particular attention to the situation across the frontier because the French High Command at Saigon had very little contact with their forces in Laos, and we should be the only sure means of getting information from that region as well as of sending help into it. I was to signal to G.H.Q. a weekly 'sitrep' covering the whole of my command, and for this purpose I was given, in addition to my wireless link with Bangkok, direct links with my sub-stations at Naung Khai and Mukdahan. We were forbidden to undertake any operations in Laos without the General's express authority, except for the purpose of smuggling arms and supplies to the French and succouring their sick and wounded.

Theoretically I was responsible for an enormous area, comprising some fifty thousand square miles and well over five hundred miles of frontier, from the sixteenth parallel to the northern border; we had hoped to establish a new sub-station in the north, opposite the Laotian capital of Luang Prabang, but SEAC vetoed the idea, thus confining our effective influence to the vicinity of the three existing missions. We were the only British forces in the country north and east of Korat[1]; and so was able to convince the General that I should need a few more officers and wireless operators.

To Naung Khai, therefore, I sent Captain Hubart, a young officer who had won the D.S.O. as an agent in France; Ubon, although within my territory, was too far from the frontier to require our close attention. Maynard

---

[1] Most of 7th Indian Division was concentrated around Bangkok and in the south. ALFPMO maintained a few missions in southern Siam and Cambodia.

was posted from Mukdahan to Nakorn Panom to act as my second-in-command and deputy in my absence; Cox unfortunately I lost, for he was needed urgently in Cambodia. In their places Major Victor Wemyss and Captain Harry Despagne took over the station at Mukdahan. Despagne, like Hubart, had won a D.S.O. in France; Wemyss, having managed tin mines in Siam before the war, knew the country and the language. He proved an admirable intelligence officer, able, hard-working and quietly efficient, although he sometimes shocked his more sensitive acquaintances by his rugged earthy manner of speaking. He was a fine natural drinker, with a head that no type or quantity of alcohol could turn, and every visit of his to my headquarters was an occasion for a special party; the next morning he would appear at our breakfast table, a little green in the face, to complain to the company: 'My God! I feel as though a whole Portuguese family just moved out of my mouth.'

During my fortnight's stay I had time to relax and absorb the glamorous and corrupting atmosphere of this gaudy, fetid and fantastic capital. Bangkok was a startling contrast of extravagance and poverty, squalor and splendour. There were broad, clean, well-paved streets lined with tall, fresh-fronted shops and blocks of flats; palaces and temples whose graceful curling roofs gleamed gaily with tiles of red and green; and pagodas whose soaring spirals threw back the sunlight in sheets of dazzling gold. There were other streets that were narrow lanes of mud and filth between rows of festering hovels with sacking hung across the doorways; and stinking canals on whose stagnant waters huddled the miserable sampan dwellings where the crowded Annamese families sweated and starved in indigence and ordure.

To my shame I must confess that I ignored the seamy side and, in the company of Smiley and other friends, devoted my spare time to the full enjoyment of this novel life. Almost every evening there was a reception or dinner party given by some Siamese notable, or a cocktail party in an Army mess. There was a variety of gay and noisy night-clubs, each providing a band, a wide selection of pretty, doll-like hostesses and an inexhaustible supply of the local whisky—a rice spirit coloured and pleasantly flavoured with brown sugar and labelled 'Mekhong' or 'Black and White Cat'. Diluted with soda-water it gave a satisfying and lasting glow for the evening, and left no hangover the next morning beyond an indefinable feeling of tension around the eyes; prolonged indulgence, however, induced a noticeable shake, increasing in some officers to the appearance of locomotor ataxia.

The little Siamese dance-hostesses took a liberal view of their duties, and after closing time were happy to extend more intimate favours to their clients. This practice caused a certain headstrong young officer in my hotel a moment of acute embarrassment. Arriving back in his room very late at the end of a bibulous evening in the night-club across the road, he suddenly realized that he had with him not one but two girls. It was, of course, strictly against standing orders for an officer to bring any woman to his room; but such puritanical restrictions made no sense to the simple minds of the Siamese hotel staff, who turned a blind eye to their infringement. My friend therefore found himself faced with a delicate problem: he had sobered up enough to realize that he was in no condition to deal with two girls; yet he could not send one of them away without giving grave offence. His solution has always seemed to me a masterpiece of tact and ingenuity. He signed to them both to strip; having made his own choice and waved her towards his bed, he gently led the other girl down the corridor to a room he knew to be occupied by a very senior visiting officer. He knocked loudly and, hearing a gruff and sleepy voice from within, opened the door a fraction and propelled his companion through into the darkness; then he softly closed the door and returned to his own room. There were, he assured me, no complaints.

Among the gayest and most hospitable of our Siamese friends was a middle-aged nobleman who had rendered valuable and hazardous service to the Allies during the Japanese occupation. A fervent Anglophile—he had lived in England before the war—he took pleasure in entertaining his British friends in Bangkok with lavish generosity and tireless exuberance. He would invite three or four of us to dinner, usually in some house on the distant outskirts of the city either owned or rented by himself to which he would drive us in his own car. There we would find awaiting our enjoyment not only plenty of food and drink but a selection of ravishing girls. That these last were designed, in the words of Gibbon, for use rather than ostentation he left us in no possible doubt. When a decent interval had elapsed after the end of the meal he would somehow manage to fade unnoticed from the party and drive himself away, leaving each of his guests deliciously stranded, like Ulysses on Calypso's island, with a glamorous and enthusiastic partner.

The girls were not prostitutes; they would take no money from us, but gave themselves over with uninhibited abandon to the pleasures of the night. Their attitude was not untypical, in my experience, of the Siamese outlook on sex which seemed to be compounded of equal parts of sensuality and humour.

There was in Bangkok a thriving business in pornography of the 'feelthy pictures' type; but what to my mind distinguished those pictures from the majority of their land was the blatant cheerfulness on the faces of the protagonists and their manifest delight in the pastime at which they were being photographed.

I was lucky to be given a room in the Ratanakosin hotel, a luxurious modern building on the main street, supposedly reserved for senior officers and distinguished civilians. It was in theory run by the government, in practice by a very attractive young Siamese receptionist whose name, as well as I can spell it, was An-Kna. She spoke perfect English and adopted towards her younger military guests an attitude of amused and sympathetic tolerance. To a friend of mine who came to inquire for me she replied with only the faintest flicker of a smile:

'If you mean Round-the-Bend Kemp, he is in.'

I flew back to Nakorn Panom at the end of November. My work during the rest of the year differed little from that of previous months, except that there was more of it. There were no Japanese troops to disarm; on the other hand the activity across the frontier was increasing and scarcely a day passed without a clash between French and Annamese or Free Lao forces. I spent much of my time on the road visiting Naung Khai and Mukdahan, but my job was made much easier for me by the enthusiasm of my staff and the confidence in us shown by General Evans, who was content to leave most decisions to me, within the framework of his original directive.

Unhappily, relations rapidly deteriorated between Captain Tavernier and the Governor of Nakorn Panom. There was certainly justification for Tavernier's repeated complaints that the Siamese authorities were giving aid and comfort to the Viet-minh; but it was seldom possible to find proof to support them. All I could do was to remonstrate with the Governor, listen as patiently as I could to his transparently false denials and counter-accusations, and relay to G.H.Q. an account of each incident; for this reason my popularity in Nakorn Panom began to wane. It is difficult to say whether the provocative behaviour of the Siamese was due to a resurgence of their old suspicion of France or to the left-wing sympathies of the Government in Bangkok; but it was a short-sighted policy, for which the French were quick to take reprisals as soon as they regained control of Thakhek.

Meanwhile Franco-Laotian soldiers visiting their friends or relatives in Nakorn Panom disappeared without trace or, when returning by *pirogue*, were intercepted and kidnapped in Siamese waters; if we ever heard of them again it was to learn that they had been beheaded. Ambushes were laid for us on Siamese territory; there was an ugly moment one evening, while we were sitting out on our veranda after dinner, when we were sniped on from the darkness, which resulted in my spilling a glassful of good Indo-Chinese rum over my newly washed, khaki drill slacks. We suffered no casualties, however, for the shooting was wild and our enemies never pressed an attack. I sometimes wondered if the object was not simply to embitter our relations with the local authorities and alarm Bangkok; the police were noticeably reluctant to pursue investigations.

Morally I was not in a very strong position to complain. For a long time I had treasured hopes of revenge upon the murderers of Klotz; against Le Hoq Minh and his subordinate, Tu, in particular, I nursed a blinding hatred and spent much of my time working on schemes for their assassination. Both, I knew, crossed often to the Siamese bank of the river, and I had information that Le Hoq Minh made periodic visits to Bangkok; if only I could get accurate information in advance it should be possible to intercept them when they passed through my territory. Having laid hands on them with the help of a few of my officers and N.C.O.s, I planned to transport them to Ban Tung and leave them to the justice of Tavernier; if that should prove impossible we would kill them and throw the bodies in the river. I suppose I must seem no better myself than the men I was pursuing, but so bitter was my hatred for those two that I could not feel I was contravening the teachings of my education and religion.

In Bangkok I had managed to obtain cautious and unofficial approval of the idea, provided I could carry it out without attracting too much attention from the Siamese. The difficulty, of course, was to get the necessary information in time. Tavernier, who was naturally enthusiastic, put his own agents at my disposal, and one day we had our chance.

I learned that Le Hoq Minh was to pass through Nakorn Panom on the following evening; the message, which was from a highly reliable source, gave enough details to make it easy for me to intercept him. I immediately sent a 'Most Urgent' signal to Bangkok, asking permission to carry out the operation. Back came their refusal, in one word of cabalese. 'Unoffbump.'

On 1st January 1946 the peace treaty was signed between the United Kingdom and Siam. The most important consequence to us was an order, a week later, to prepare for the withdrawal of all my missions. Now that they were masters in their own house the Siamese were not going to tolerate in it activities such as ours. General Evans and his superiors were no longer in a position to resist their pressure, because by now the French in Laos had begun to receive support from Saigon; moreover, the grave political consequences that would result if one of us were murdered far outweighed any value we might still possess. On 20th January I left Nakorn Panom for the last time.

My orders were to take my two parties from Nakorn Panom and Mukdahan in lorries as far as the railhead at Ubon, together with all our stores; there we were to hand over the lorries and stores to Major Hedley of the British Military Mission to the Siamese Army, and travel by train to Bangkok. The Governor and his officers saw us off from Nakorn Panom in the morning; although we parted with expressions of mutual esteem and affection they can hardly have been sorry to see us go, for our support of the French had caused them continual vexation and embarrassment. Tavernier, on the other hand, seemed genuinely distressed, even shattered; he showed little confidence in the support of his superiors at Saigon.

Ubon, about thirty miles from the frontier of Indo-China, was the headquarters of an important military district and of a division of the Siamese Army; Johnny Hedley, whom I had already met with Smiley, was living in a wing of the barracks on the outskirts of the town. A spare, sun-baked figure with unblinking light blue eyes and a slow, elaborate drawl, he gave the impression that he found all conversation tedious. He was an Old Etonian and an Old Burma Hand who had spent his happiest days in the teak forests and despised the comfort and frivolity of city life; even for official parties or government receptions in the capital he refused to vary his style of dress—a battered old bush hat, a shapeless bush shirt, slacks and jungle boots, and an old .303 Lee Enfield service rifle, which he carried slung from his shoulder or propped in a corner of the room, heedless of his hosts' astonishment, indignation or alarm. He was not always tactful with senior officers. When the Brigadier commanding his mission, an amiable old gentleman whom he had not met before, flew up to Ubon on a visit of inspection, Hedley greeted him without the formality of a salute.

'Have you brought my mail?' were his opening words.

'Er-no-er, I'm afraid I didn't bring any mail,' stammered the surprised Brigadier.

'Humph! Somebody in Bangkok ought to pull their fingers out.'

However, his welcome to us was friendly enough. There was a train leaving for Bangkok in three days' time, he explained—only a goods train, but he would fix us up with some wicker chairs in one of the waggons; in the meantime he had plenty of room for us in his quarters.

It was on the second night of our stay that a very curious incident befell me, one which might have brought my adventures to a painful end. It is fixed for ever in my memory as The Night I Lost My Trousers. We had spent most of the evening drinking and playing poker with Hedley, a young Australian captain from the War Graves Commission, and some Sappers who had arrived on a road reconnaissance of north-eastern Siam; Hedley, who drank little himself, had nevertheless laid in a large supply of Siamese whisky and Indo-Chinese rum; and we, after weeks of hard work and worry, were in the mood to relax. The party broke up about midnight, but before turning in I decided to take a short walk in the cool night to clear my head of the fumes of smoke and liquor. When the others had gone upstairs to bed I stepped outside into the darkness.

I have no idea how long afterwards it was when I came to. At first I was aware only of a splitting headache, a dim and flickering light in my eyes, and a rancid, smoky smell; the last two, I soon saw, came from an old and dirty lamp on the ground a yard away from my face. The lower part of my body felt cold and bare.

I lay still for a while, hoping the pain would go from my head and wondering apathetically where on earth I was and what had happened to bring me there. I could remember nothing after walking out of the room at the barracks, but I seemed to have a distant recollection, as though from a dream, of hearing voices whispering near me as I was regaining consciousness; but it was only the faintest impression, perhaps no more than imagination. Very slowly I opened my eyes; painfully I raised myself on an elbow and looked around.

I was lying on a heap of filthy sacking on the floor of a squalid, smoke-filled peasant's hovel, bare of any kind of furniture. I was quite alone, and my loneliness and the dark, empty silence around me began to fill me with a frightening sense of desolation and foreboding. Then fear gave way to astonishment as I saw the reason for the chilly feeling round my lower limbs. I was still wearing the bush shirt I had put on before dinner, but below the waist I was naked; my trousers, underpants, socks and shoes had vanished. I looked carefully round the room, but could see no place where they might be hidden. Desperately I tried to concentrate and remember what had happened.

My last clear memory was of walking out of that room at the barracks. Was it possible that during my walk in the fresh air I had picked up or been picked up by some woman? I quickly decided that I was safe in rejecting that explanation; I might have had too much to drink, but certainly not so much that I should have forgotten all about it if it had happened. Had I, then, been robbed? I examined the pockets of my bush shirt. My wallet was still there, stuffed with money, and so were my military identity card and all my documents; even my wrist watch was intact. The pockets of my missing trousers had contained nothing more than an old pipe and tobacco pouch. Evidently I had not fallen among thieves.

Reluctantly I forced myself to stand up, ignoring the stabbing pains in my head, and padded barefoot round the room in search of my missing clothes. There was no sign of them; the hut had only one room and only one door, which opened out into the darkness of the night. I returned to my pile of sacking and tried to think again.

I was now quite sure that, whatever had brought on my loss of memory, it was more than mere excess of alcohol; apart from a headache and a cloudy mind I had none of the symptoms that usually attend a hangover. And then I remembered: I knew just when I had last felt like this. In August 1943 I had parachuted into Albania; the pilot had dropped me too late and I had landed half-way up the side of a mountain, knocking myself out on a boulder as I fell. When I regained consciousness it was with this same muzzy, disembodied feeling and a similar gap in my memory.

This train of thought had unpleasant implications. Had I simply fallen down outside the barracks and hit my head on a stone—in which case why wasn't I back there in my own bed? Or had I been slugged on the head and—I began to tremble—kidnapped? At this point I was interrupted by a shuffling sound outside the door of the hut. Naked and unarmed—for I had left my pistol at the barracks—I cowered back on the sacking to await the intruder; all my courage had evaporated in my humiliation, embarrassment and alarm.

He was an ancient peasant, bent and emaciated, with a wrinkled, yellow-brown face; the bones of his ribs and chest showed skeleton c ear through his skin above the dirty white and grey chequered loincloth that was all his clothing. He sidled slowly across the floor and bent over the lamp, his face expressionless, while I watched him through half-closed eyes. When I saw he was alone; whispered good evening in Siamese, forcing an ingratiating smile. His reaction was hardly reassuring. He turned on me a brief, hostile look and padded swiftly from the room.

Pain and dizziness forgotten, I was on my feet in an instant. I was thoroughly frightened. Whoever had brought me to this hut had not done so for the good of my health; if, as seemed likely, the old peasant had gone to tell them I was awake, they would not be long in returning. It was then that I remembered the Viet-minh and the price on my head.

Nothing so concentrates a man's mind, observed Dr. Johnson, as the knowledge that he is going to be hanged. My own mind instantly became clear: I must get away from this hut, and quickly. Shivering with disgust I snatched up a piece of the sacking I had been lying on, and wrapped it round my middle. I padded across the earthen floor to the doorway and peered cautiously outside. There was no sign of a guard. With a muttered prayer I plunged, for the second time that night, into the darkness.

There was no challenge or sound of pursuit as I ran blindly on in my terrified resolve to put as much distance as I could between myself and that sinister hut. After a few minutes I stopped for breath and took a quick look around, trying to get my bearings. There was no moon, but the bright stars gave a little light. I had no idea where I was, nor how far or in which direction lay the barracks. The only plan I could think of was to continue walking, taking a rough course from the stars, until I should come upon some familiar landmark or some lights that might show me the way.

Hitherto I had been too frightened to worry about anything except my escape; but now, as I plodded on in my bare feet, I began to think of snakes and scorpions and to strain my eyes in an effort to see what I was treading on. I padded forward with infinite caution, shuddering in anticipation each time I put my foot to the ground.

Every few minutes I halted and crouched down to listen for sounds of pursuit. Once I heard the hum of muffled voices getting rapidly louder. I froze in terror until I realized they were coming from the opposite direction; even so, I decided to take no chances, and kept down until they had passed out of earshot.

I had been going about twenty minutes when I heard a new sound behind me; the clink and clatter of arms and accoutrements. A party of police or soldiers was approaching, and for the first time in that ghastly evening I felt a surge of hope; in all probability they were making for the barracks. Of course it would never do for them to find a British officer of field rank wandering about the countryside at half past one in the morning without his trousers; but there was no reason why I should not let them overtake me and then follow them home at a discreet distance. As they drew closer I crouched low on the ground, holding my breath and praying that they would not see me. However, they loped past within a few yards, chattering unconcernedly in their high, sing-song voices. I rose to my feet and followed them silently, keeping my eyes fixed on their dim silhouettes and forgetting at last the dangers of snakes and scorpions.

It must have been ten minutes later, though it seemed an hour, when I saw in front of us a line of lights and recognized them as the barracks. I almost cried out in my relief. I let my guides draw ahead to a safe distance, and made my way cautiously towards the buildings until I had picked out the wing where we were billeted.

I paused for a moment to make sure there were no sentries around, and to collect what remained of my courage; then, with a prayer on my lips, I girded my sackcloth-encased limbs and sprinted across the barrack square. In a few seconds I was through the doorway out of which I had sauntered so carelessly an hour or two—or was it a year or two?—earlier. I raced up the stairs and collapsed on my bed, shaking and sweating with exertion and relief. Suddenly I began to laugh, hysterically and uncontrollably, until the tears poured down my face. I had just remembered the code name of my mission: 'Sackcloth'.

My companions received my story the next morning with a mixture of incredulity and delight; they produced several theories to account for it, the simplest and by far the most popular being that I had left my trousers in a brothel. Hedley alone looked thoughtful.

'We'd better find that hut,' was his comment.

But we never did find it. In the first place I could not be certain how far or in what direction it lay; secondly, there were any number of peasant huts of the same description in the neighborhood. Much later, however, from discreet inquiries of the Siamese authorities and from some fragments of information I picked up in Bangkok I pieced together the story of what must have happened that night. Although the details are largely surmise the outline seems pretty certain; in which case I am indeed lucky to be alive.

It seems that Viet-minh agents had been keeping us under observation even at Ubon. When I stepped outside for my breath of air, one—or more probably two—of them had spotted me. Seeing a chance of collecting the large reward offered for me, they had knocked me on the back of the neck— I had wondered why there was no bump on my head—and dragged me away. It would have been too risky for them to murder me on the spot, but easy to drag me off to the hut. Probably they bribed or frightened the driver of a bullock cart into taking us to his hut; or perhaps the hut belonged to one of their sympathizers. It is impossible to say.

In the hut they were faced with a dilemma. In order to collect the reward they would have to hand me over to the Viet-minh, preferably alive; but there was no one at hand competent to take delivery of my body. They must therefore have decided to leave me in the care of the old peasant while they went to find the local Viet-minh commander. Presumably they had no rope, or they would have tied me up; instead they took away my trousers and shoes in the belief that I should be unable to move very far without them.

Obviously something upset their plans. Perhaps the Viet-minh commander was away; or the old peasant took fright when he saw that I had recovered, and fled without warning them; or perhaps they themselves lost their nerve. Whatever the reason, I am heartily thankful for it; I have heard too many stories of Viet-minh irregulars disembowelling their prisoners.

My intention had been to apply at once for the demobilization to which I was now entitled. But while waiting in Bangkok I was offered and immediately accepted the command of a mission to the islands of Bali and Lombok in the Netherlands East Indies. There the Japanese garrisons had not yet surrendered, and the situation in both islands was obscure; SEAC therefore decided to send in a small advance party of British troops before committing the Dutch forces of occupation. On 15th February I flew to Singapore; two days later I was in Java.

V

JAVA

Bright sunlight, soft breezes and a blaze of tropical greenery was the picture I had formed of the islands of Indonesia, described by the Dutch writer Multatuli as 'a girdle of emerald around the Equator'. Reality, when I stood forlornly beside the sodden runway of Batavia[1] airport at half past ten on the morning of 17th February, was grotesquely different. A thick, warm curtain of rain, falling from a blanket of puffy grey clouds and whipped across the airfield by the violence of the monsoon, blotted out the horizon and drained all colour from trees and grass and buildings. My fellow-passengers from the Dakota were driven away to their various units, leaving me standing in the open—bewildered, dripping and alone.

After a quarter of an hour an open jeep splashed up, driven by an apologetic young subaltern who took me to the Hotel des Indes, a large sprawling building once the queen of hotels in the Far East. War and the ensuing emergency had deprived it of its former extravagant splendour. Gone were the enormous meals of *rijsttafel*, each requiring a posse of fifteen waiters to carry the dishes, which had sent so many colonial administrators and business men to their early graves; and the high, airy suites with their wide verandas were stripped of most of their furniture and crowded with extra beds.

The situation in the capital was quiet but tense. Troops were required to carry arms in the streets, there was a strict curfew at midnight, and some quarters of the town and port were out of bounds; but the hours of daylight generally passed without incident. The nights were full of danger for the foolhardy; almost every morning patrols would retrieve from the drainage canals the dismembered bodies of British or Indian soldiers who had defied the curfew in search of liquor or women; girls indeed made a practice of enticing troops into their houses to be set upon by their menfolk.

The sudden end to the war brought about by the bombs on Hiroshima and Nagasaki found South-East Asia Command quite unprepared for the problems of policing and administration that immediately followed. For the Dutch East Indies, which had only been placed within the British sphere of operations by the Potsdam conference in July, there were scarcely any troops available. In Java the nationalists, encouraged by Japanese propaganda during

---

[1] Now called Jakarta, the capital of the Netherlands East Indies was at the time still known by its old Dutch name of Batavia.

the occupation and armed after the surrender by the Japanese Sixteenth Army on the orders of its commander, seized control of most of the country, proclaimed their independence and organized a provincial government under the leadership of Dr. Sukarno. With their own demand for freedom they identified, illogically, their claim to sovereignty over all the peoples of Indonesia, many of whom differed widely in language, religion and culture from the Moslem Javanese, of whose influence they were bitterly resentful and afraid. The various nationalist groups, many of them little more than robber bands admitting no loyalty to the Sukarno government—they included the Communists under the Moscow-trained Tan Malaka—were united only in their hostility to the Dutch and to the British, who attempted to restore order in the Dutch name.

British and Indian reinforcements landed and, by the time I arrived, had secured perimeters defending the towns of Batavia, Buitenzorg, Bandaung, Semarang and Surabaja.[1] Only between Batavia and Buitenzorg was communication possible by road, and then only in convoys, which often had to fight their way through ambushes at a heavy cost in casualties. The nationalists did not spare their prisoners, whom they usually put to death by hewing in pieces to the greater glory of *Merdeka*;[2] a risk which added to the hazards of a forced landing when flying over that jungle-covered, mountainous and enchantingly beautiful country.

Tolerance and mercy are qualities seldom found in twentieth century revolutionaries. Towards their own people the Javanese nationalists behaved with extreme ruthlessness, maintaining their grip upon the countryside by an effective apparatus of terror. For example, they forbade the peasants, on pain of death, to trade with the Allies or even to possess the guilders issued as currency by the Allied military administration. Villagers who lived near towns occupied by the Allies were faced with the alternatives of defying the ban, or letting their produce rot and starving themselves; most of them chose to trade, and many were executed for it by their liberators. But the full fury of Javanese chauvinism was reserved for the Eurasians. Devotedly loyal to the Dutch Crown—they provided some of the best officers of the R.N.E.I. Army and some of the ablest officials in the administration—those unfortunate people, wherever the nationalists were in control, fell victims to barbaric persecution and atrocious massacre.

Formerly among the richest countries of Asia, with a happy and prosperous people, Java in 1946 presented a melancholy spectacle of

---

[1] The Royal Netherlands East Indies Army, destroyed by the Japanese, was being slowly reconstituted with Dutch, Eurasian, and native troops from the prisoner-of-war camps throughout South-East Asia.

[2] The nationalist slogan. Malay for that much abused word, Freedom.

neglected paddy-fields and derelict plantations abandoned by an impoverished and terrified peasantry.

Two days later, in the warm, wet darkness before dawn, I stood once again on Batavia airport, talking to the crew of the Dakota which was to fly me to Surabaja on the next stage of my journey. The general nature of my mission had been explained to me at AFNEI[1] Headquarters: to lead a small British reconnaissance party to Bali, and afterwards to Lombok, and prepare for the landing of the main occupation force, which would be Dutch. We should go in by sea. The operation would be under the direct control of General Mansergh, commanding 5th Indian Division at Surabaja, who would brief me in detail.

With me was my second-in-command, Captain John Shaw, attached to me from the staff of SEAC Intelligence. Shaw and I had trained together at Weedon in 1940, after which he had joined the Royal Horse Guards in Palestine and won the M.C. in the Syrian campaign. A tall, solidly built Yorkshireman, he combined a placid, easy-going attitude with a sound knowledge of his job, shrewd common sense and a thorough attention to detail. Often in the next two months I was to praise the good fortune that had brought us together. In addition to his many other duties, he performed with conscientious efficiency and patience the exacting task of getting his erratic commanding officer to the right place at the right time.

We were joined on the airfield by a party of three Japanese officers, led by a Major-General Ando; he was a short, slight, solemn man with a fussy but deferential manner. He had with him a major and a lieutenant interpreter. They were coming with us to make the first contacts with the Japanese garrisons of the islands and to act as liaison officers. We never came to know them well because our orders forbade any but the most formal relations with them—we were expressly forbidden even to shake hands with them or any of their countrymen; but they carried out our instructions faithfully and proved themselves invaluable on both operations.

We took off into the sunrise in a lull between the rainstorms and flew along the coast, gazing at the flattened cones of the great volcanoes that rose out of the jungle against the southern skyline. After a brief halt for breakfast at Semarang we landed at half past ten at Surabaja. Until a few days previously the Indonesians had been able to sweep the airfield with small-arms fire; now they had been pushed back, but they could still shell the runway, and I was relieved when we had taxied safely to the dispersal point and were driven off in a large green Chevrolet to Divisional Headquarters in the centre of the town.

---

[1] Allied Forces Netherlands East Indies, at that time under the command of General Sir Montague Stopford.

Surabaja at the end of the previous October had been the scene of some of the bloodiest fighting against the Indonesians. At that time the only Allied force there was rather less than one brigade of 23rd Indian Division, deployed in the dock area under the command of that very fine and gallant soldier, Brigadier Mallaby. While attempting to negotiate the release of a large number of Dutch and Eurasians interned in the town, the Brigadier was murdered by a hysterical crowd of Indonesians. This incident was the signal for a general attack on his brigade, which, hopelessly outnumbered in men and weapons, was only saved from annihilation by the arrival of General Mansergh's 5th Indian Division, hurriedly transported from Singapore; even so, one battalion was wiped out; brigade headquarters was overrun, and every man in it slaughtered. Several hundred Eurasian men, women and children were hideously butchered in the lavatories of the Officers' Club.

Mansergh immediately issued an ultimatum to the Indonesian leaders to hand over the rest of the internees and to lay down their arms. When they refused he launched a full-scale assault with artillery, tanks and aircraft. He was only just in time: the Indonesians had herded their Dutch and Eurasian prisoners—some sixteen hundred men, women and children—into the prison, and were pouring petrol over the roof and walls preparatory to burning them alive. Mansergh opened fire on the prison with an anti-tank gun loaded with armour-piercing shot; through the narrow hole blasted in the wall a company of an Indian regiment entered two abreast, shot down the Indonesians who were in the act of setting fire to the building, and freed the prisoners. Nearly three weeks of bitter fighting followed before the town was cleared. A fortnight later Mansergh and his officers had the civil administration, the public services and even the schools functioning—a remarkable achievement in the face of repeated Indonesian attacks on the perimeter defences.

We met with a most friendly welcome from Colonel Carroll, the GI, who had planned our operation, and the G2, Major Armour. They apologized charmingly for the temporary absence of the General.

'At the moment he's out on the perimeter inspecting some new positions. He spends most of his time out there, poking around the hot spots. The troops think the world of him, but he causes us a lot of worry.'

We were to embark in three days' time aboard H.M. Frigate *Loch Eck* (Lieut.-Commander Peter Hoare, R.N.), now lying in the harbour, and we should arrive off the port of Benoa in South Bali on the morning of the 23rd. The Dutch force would land exactly a week later. Our party would consist of an escort of eight Buffs under a sergeant; six signallers with two wireless sets; an R.A.M.C. sergeant and a naval officer, Lieutenant Neville, who was a qualified beachmaster; he was, in a way, the most important member of the mission, because the Dutch force was to land in assault craft on to an open beach.

My first task would be to accept the formal surrender of the Japanese naval and military garrisons; my second to establish law and order and some sort of administration in the island, and my third to deploy the Japanese forces to cover the beachhead and the Dutch landing. I should have to rely on the Japanese for the maintenance of security; it was assumed they would be prepared to surrender and place themselves under my orders. The most uncertain factors were the attitude of the Balinese population and the strength of nationalist feeling among them; my report on these points would be of especial interest to 5th Indian Division.

'In other words,' Armour concluded cheerfully, 'if they chop you up we'll know we'll have to be more careful with the next lot.'

The following morning we met the Divisional Commander. General Mansergh was a widely experienced soldier of about forty-five who had greatly distinguished himself with the Fourteenth Army in Burma. He was an impressive figure, tall and broad-shouldered, with an alert intelligent face, firm features and an easy, informal manner; to me he always conveyed the feeling that he had every situation or eventuality under perfect control. Towards his subordinates he was invariably courteous and sympathetic, and he earned every bit of the affection and respect in which they held him.

When he was satisfied that we understood all the points of his plan he said to me:

'Until the Dutch arrive you chaps frankly are going to be out on a limb; there's little we can do to help you if you get into trouble. You will be my representative and, through me, the representative of the Supreme Allied Commander; as such you must make it quite clear from the start to the Japanese and to the locals that your orders are to be obeyed implicitly. There is one point which is vitally important; no word must leak out that the main landing will be carried out by the Dutch. You must not reveal this information even to the Japanese commanders, and you must impress on all your party the need for absolute security. It is essential that the landing should take place without opposition, but there may well be trouble from the locals if they hear that the Dutch are coming. If you're asked about the composition of the main landing force you will say that they will be Allied troops, but you don't know what nationality. Is that clear?

'Another point: you may well have to resort to force to keep order, and you have plenty of it in the shape of the Japanese, if you need it. But I do ask you to use it only as a last resort. There's a great deal of opposition in certain quarters at home to our role here in the N.E.I.—they say we're using troops to bolster up Dutch colonialism; whenever I have to give orders to clear out a nest of snipers that's been harassing my men I seem to feel the hot, angry breath of Socialism on the back of my neck. So for God's sake be careful how you use the Japanese in Bali. Of course you will keep in close touch with me through your wireless, but, as the man on the spot, you will have to make most of the decisions yourself. Keep me informed. I will back you up.' And so he did.

Shaw collected our stores from Colonel Waddilove, the A.Q., and supervised their lodging aboard *Loch Eck* Waddilove and his assistant, the Judian Major Kannah, went out of their way to provide us with everything we could possibly need, including fifteen gallons of 'operational rum' and plenty of beer and whisky.

I spent most of my time plaguing General Mansergh's hard-worked but ever helpful staff officers for information about the topography, history and politics of Bali.

I had long talks with the commander of the Dutch landing force, Colonel Ter Meulen, a bluff, amiable veteran of the R.N.E.I. Army who had commanded its 'Bali Korps' in pre-war days; unlike most of his troops, who had recently emerged from Japanese prison camps, he had been captured in Holland in 1940. He flattered me by listening to my suggestions with a respect he can scarcely have felt. His Intelligence Officer, Captain Daan Hubrecht, was a delightful and uninhibited eccentric. The son of a Cambridge astronomy professor who had also served as Dutch Minister in Rome and Madrid and who owned large sugar estates in east Java, Hubrecht had benefited from the most liberal cosmopolitan education and upbringing of anyone I have known; a handsome, carefree person of unusual intelligence, sensitivity and charm he had taken his Degree at Trinity and his pleasures in the sophisticated pre-war society of the major European capitals. Coming east to enter the family business in Surabaja he had immediately responded to the proximity and lure of Bali; in the course of frequent and protracted visits he had fallen in love with the island and its beautiful, fascinating people. Three years of captivity in Changi gaol in Singapore had sharpened his anxiety to return. His knowledge of Malay—the *lingua franca* of the Archipelago—his experience and his popularity with the Balinese made him during the next three months an indispensable and most stimulating companion.

We boarded *Loch Eck* on the 21st, after a lively farewell lunch with Carroll, Waddilove and Armour, at which one of our fellow guests, I remember, was the intrepid Colonel Laurens Van Der Post. In the evening, when we had seen our party settled into their accommodation and the three Japanese quartered in a petty officers' mess—to the indignation of the evicted P.O.s.— Commander Hoare invited us to drinks in the wardroom. This short, bearded, energetic sailor had the reputation of a martinet with his officers but, like them, was unfailingly hospitable and helpful to us. We were to sail at dawn, but in the midst of all this festivity I found it difficult to realize that I was entrusted with a complicated mission whose failure would cost many more lives than my own.

At least, I reflected, we could not have asked for more co-operation and support than we had received from 5th Indian Division. At this point perhaps

I should mention one item of our stores that was later to cause me considerable embarrassment. Pointing out that I was responsible for the health as well as the safety of my party the A.D.M.S.[1] I had insisted on handing to me, over and above the supply carried by our medical sergeant, several gross of those contraceptives usually known as French letters. They were thrust into the pockets of my rucksack and forgotten. Soon after my return to London I was invited to tea by a much loved aunt, who also asked me to bring along my rucksack, which she wished to borrow for her son to take on a holiday in Switzerland. Only when I was in the taxi on my way to her house did I remember what that rucksack still contained. Useless, I knew, to attempt any explanation. Sweating with anxiety and keeping a furtive eye on the driver, I lowered each of the spare passenger seats in turn, loaded it with the contents of the pockets and gently released it to its normal position, where it effectively concealed them. I have often wondered about the reactions of the driver and his next fare.

---

[1] Assistant Director of Medical Services.

VI

ARRIVAL IN BALI

Closed up at action stations *Loch Eck* steamed safely past the Indonesian batteries commanding the narrow strait between Madura and the mainland. Afterwards I strolled on deck watching the mountains of Java slip slowly by, distant grey outlines in the muggy haze. Our troops seemed to look forward to the venture with a mixture of mild curiosity and amusement; they showed no signs either of excitement or anxiety. The Buffs, very brisk and soldierly and very young—the oldest was their sergeant, not yet twenty—were invariably cheerful and gave an impressive display of smartness and efficiency on all ceremonial occasions; the signallers, much less tidy, took full advantage of their traditional right to grumble, but also put into their work all their traditional skill and energy. The father of the party was Sergeant Hopkins, R.A.M.C., a grizzled old regular soldier of inexhaustible patience and good humour; such was the men's respect for him that during the two operations we only had one case of sickness—a mild attack of bronchitis.

I was awakened early on the morning of the 23rd by the lowering of the anchor; we were lying in Benoa Roads, a mile off the tiny harbour built by the Dutch which is the only port in South Bali. About half past seven a Japanese landing-craft drew alongside, under the command of an ugly little naval lieutenant who told us sourly that Sixteenth Army had omitted to warn the garrison of our arrival. We sent Ando's party ashore to tell the commanders that we should land in the afternoon for an unofficial visit of inspection.

Another landing-craft came for us at noon. With Peter Hoare, Shaw, Neville and the Buffs escort I took my place in the stern and prepared for my meeting with the officers whom we could see awaiting us on the jetty; I wondered anxiously if we were right in our easy assumption that they would obey me, or if our reception was going to be warm rather than friendly.

It was a fair afternoon with a soft, fresh breeze to temper the midday heat; the sun sparkled on the clear blue water and struck bright on the limestone cliffs of the bare Tafelhoek peninsula as we nosed our way slowly between the double line of buoys that marked the channel through the hidden coral reefs. Ahead of us lay a beach of dazzling white sand, rising in a gentle slope to a fringe of palm trees whose foliage gleamed a startling vivid green against the indigo shadow of the hinterland.

A company of infantry was drawn up on the jetty. As we stepped ashore there was a bellowed command, the officers' swords flashed in salute, and with smart precision the troops presented arms; returning the salute I reflected that now at least we were over the first fence. There followed a brief conference with Captain Okuyama, the senior naval officer, who was in command of the garrison, and his military colleague, Colonel Tsuneoka; Okuyama was a short, grizzled officer of dignified bearing with intelligent, sensitive features. They had brought with them their own interpreter, Miura, a smooth and shifty-looking official of the Japanese Civil Affairs Administration, obsequious and spotless in a well-pressed white duck suit. I told them to report aboard *Loch Eck* at 0930 next morning to sign the terms of surrender; the full surrender ceremony would be taken by General Mansergh himself about a week after the main landing, until which time officers and men would retain their arms—at this last statement a look of profound relief crossed both commanders' faces. This relief became more pronounced as I passed on General Mansergh's instructions that my orders were to be obeyed implicitly; it began to dawn on me that these officers had not been enjoying their equivocal position of responsibility in isolation. We passed on to discuss troop concentrations and the organization of naval patrols in the Bali Strait to prevent the infiltration of terrorists from Java—a very difficult task owing to the narrowness of the strait and the length of the coastline.

A large and comfortable staff car took us the seven miles to Den Pasar, the capital of South Bali and pre-war centre of the island's tourist industry, where we were to establish our headquarters. The Japanese warned us that this town was the centre of extremist feeling, the countryside being for the moment comparatively quiet. When I asked if there had been any incidents Captain Okuyama answered in precise tones:

'On 13th December last the islanders unlawfully attacked our troops. The object of this attack was to gain possession of our arms. We suppressed the attack and detained the headmen responsible. They are now in custody.'

A great improvement on what happened in Java, I said to myself, making a mental note to visit those headmen in prison as soon as I had the time.

All along the straight tarmac road, lined with tall palms and flanked by rich green paddy-fields, we passed groups of Balinese—slight, well-built young men whose muscles rippled above their brightly coloured loincloths; slender, golden-skinned girls with firm, bare breasts; old men and women with emaciated bodies and skeleton ribs who still retained their dignified and graceful bearing, and children wide-eyed with bewilderment and surprise. Some stared at us in silent curiosity; others, especially the women and children, smiled and waved; a few of the men gave the *merdeka* salute, but hesitatingly, as though uncertain whether it was the right thing to do.

South Bali, separated from the north by a wild range of high volcanic mountains—one of them, Batur, is still active—is by far the more fertile and thickly populated part of the country; indeed it supports the great majority of the million and a half inhabitants which the Balinese genius for rice cultivation enables to live without hardship on an island of only five thousand square kilometres.[1] Den Pasar had therefore been selected for our base in preference to Singaradja, the capital; it was, moreover, close to the beach where the Dutch force was to land.

The town, covering an area no longer or broader than a man could comfortably walk in fifteen minutes, centred round a large grassy square named the Alun-Alun,[2] planted with trees along the edges and resembling a public playground—on which model, indeed, it seemed to have been designed. Around it in their trim little gardens stood the neat white bungalows of the former Dutch officials; the largest had previously been the Residency and was now the Japanese naval headquarters. To the east a road ran to the village of Sanoer and the beach where we were expecting the Dutch to land; to the west a street Lined with squalid modern shops led to the markets and the Javanese and Chinese quarters. On either side of the road leading north stood the luxurious buildings of the Bali Hotel and its annex; beyond them, surrounded by a mud wall pierced with thatched gateways lay the old Balinese village of Badung, from which the local Rajah took his title.

Leaving the Bali Hotel for Colonel Ter Meulen and his staff, we ordered the Japanese to prepare the Residency for our occupation the following afternoon; a single-storey but roomy bungalow with a large courtyard and garden at the back and a short, crescent-shaped sweep of drive in front leading from the road and the Alun-Alun, it could easily accommodate my entire party. Our last action before returning to Benoa was to requisition three staff cars from the Japanese, one each for Shaw, Neville and myself.

A light breeze ruffled the blue-green waters of Benoa Roads and swayed the feathery tops of the palm trees beyond the line of breakers on the shore; inland, dark banks of grey cloud threatened heavy rain, but overhead the morning sun beat warm upon the canvas awning spread above the frigate's quarterdeck. Even in the shade the paintwork gleamed a spotless light grey, the brass shone, the deck was holystoned to a faultless white; Commander Hoare had prepared an impressive setting for the ceremony that was about to begin.

The after bulkhead was draped with the Union Jack and Stars and Stripes; beneath the flags was ranged a line of chairs at a long table spread with a green baize cloth. Here Commander Hoare, my officers and I took our seats;

---

[1] Owing to a remarkable increase in the population since 1946 there is now, I believe, some shortage of food in Bali.

[2] The Dutch did me the honour of re-christening the Alun-Alun 'Kemp Platz', but since their departure I understand it has reverted to some more suitable and doubtless more euphonious Indonesian title.

facing us, at a short distance, was another line of chairs, as yet empty. Aft, in ceremonial white dress, were assembled the men of the ship's company; the officers, immaculate in Number Tens, lined up on our left against the starboard rail. At the gangway head, on the port side, stood Mansell, the First Lieutenant, with a Chief Petty Officer and, very impressive in their smartly pressed green uniforms and scrubbed and blancoed webbing, the armed guard party of the Buffs.

On the blotter in front of me lay a five page roneo document entitled 'Formal Instrument of Surrender', which the Japanese Commanders would have to sign. In brief, its terms empowered me to assume command of the Japanese naval and military garrison; to use Japanese forces as I thought fit for police and labour duties, in particular for the preparation and protection of the landing beaches; and to take over the civil and military administration of the island until the arrival of the Dutch. On my left Hoare was studying a shorter paper, which he would read out at the opening of the ceremony, embodying certain immediate naval requirements. Although this was to be only a formal surrender, and the official surrender of the garrison would be taken by General Mansergh after the main landing, I could not suppress a surge of pride at the thought of the small but historic role I was allowed to assume.

> Is it not passing brave to be a king,
> And ride in triumph through Persepolis?

As the time drew on to half past nine a tense, expectant silence descended on the ship; the slapping of the waves against the hull broke strangely loud on our ears.

A shout from Mansell at the gangway head announced the approach of the Japanese Surrender Commission. A few minutes later they climbed aboard—Captain Okuyama, Colonel Tsuneoka, two staff officers and the interpreter, Miura; when Mansell had relieved each officer of his sword, which he placed on a table by the gangway, the party approached us, came smartly to attention and bowed gravely to Hoare and me. In accordance with our orders from General Mansergh we remained seated, and told Mansell to lead them to their places. Followed by General Ando and his two officers, they sat down facing us.

When Hoare and I had read out the surrender terms Okuyama asked our permission to withdraw and discuss them with his colleague; Mansell led them to Hoare's cabin. Half an hour later they returned to tell us they would sign. Each of them came up to the table, affixed his signature in ink with a thin brush, and sat down. While Hoare was dictating to Miura final orders for our disembarkation that afternoon, I happened to glance at Okuyama. He was sitting quite still with his hands upon his knees, his head bowed and his lined old face puckered in grief; tears dripped slowly down his shrunken cheeks. As I watched him my heart was filled with an overwhelming pity, and the glamour and glory of my position faded to a shadow. Perhaps I ought not to put my feelings on record for I had suffered nothing at the hands of the Japanese. Their callousness and cruelty, the brutality of their prison camps, and the horrors of the Burma-Siam railway were things I had heard of but not experienced. I had never met Japanese in battle, the most I had had to do was keep out of their way. Now in my unearned hour of triumph I felt ashamed to watch this veteran sailor, who had spent his life in a service with a great fighting tradition, weeping openly over his humiliation at the hands of a jumped-up young lieutenant-colonel who had never even fought against him.

We disembarked that afternoon, and by the evening had established ourselves in the Residency; *Loch Eck* remained at anchor off Benoa for another twenty-four hours with a landing-party ready to come to our assistance if we should fire a Verey light. We posted a pair of sentries on the gates in front of the house, more for the sake of appearances than from fear of attack. Whatever undercurrents of hostility might be flowing beneath the surface, there had so far been nothing but friendliness in our welcome from the Balinese; nevertheless I ordered Colonel Tsuneoka to station a platoon of infantry on the Alun-Alun to cover our headquarters against a sudden attack. Our signallers installed their equipment in the entrance hall of the Residency, and before midnight I had sent my first message to 5th Indian Division.

While Shaw and Sergeant Hopkins busied themselves with the accommodation of our troops and the stowage of our stores, I sat down in the office which had been prepared for me in the front of the house to study the intelligence reports I had received from the Japanese and compare them with the information I had collected Surabaja. From time to time, as the night wore on, we went outside and stood listening in the heavy, scented air for any sound of trouble from the town; we heard nothing but the soft tread of the sentries m their rubber-soled canvas boots. Those young men seemed strangely indifferent to their lonely situation in a strange and possibly hostile island.

I was still at my desk when dawn broke. I was appalled at the amount of work that lay ahead of us in the short time before the arrival of the main force, and at the loss of life that would follow any failure or mistake on my part. The civil administration of the island was in chaos, and I should have to build it up from scratch; the few Balinese officials who remained at their posts were, it appeared, too frightened of the extremists to give us any help or even advice.[1] The beaches where the Dutch proposed to land were at present unfit for any craft much larger than a canoe; we should need a considerable Japanese labour force to prepare them for D Day, and we must deploy other Japanese formations to cover the landings. There was a disused airstrip at Kuta in the south of the island, which we were required to make serviceable for Dakotas. Lastly, and of prime importance, I must find out the strength of the extremists, especially around Den Pasar, and, if possible, the names of their leaders; and I must make contact immediately with a number of influential Balinese who, I had been told, were well disposed towards us and capable of assuming the responsibilities of government.

I had heard that there were three Europeans still at large on the island, all of them artists: the well-known Belgian painter, Le Mayeur, who lived with his Balinese wife at Sanoer; the Austrian Strasser, somewhere in the mountains of the north, and an eccentric Swiss, Theo Meier, whose house was near Selat in eastern Bali among the foothills of the great volcano, Gunung Agung. They should be able to give us valuable and unprejudiced information about local conditions.

There would be little rest or even sleep for any of us, I reflected; but at least I was fortunate in being able to delegate with confidence much of the work to my officers. Over breakfast the three of us discussed the situation. I decided to concentrate on the political problems; Neville would be responsible for the beaches, Shaw for the airstrip. The tactical disposition of the Japanese formations to cover the landings was, of course, my personal responsibility; but Shaw, who had much more experience of tactics in this war than I, undertook to work out the details with Colonel Tsuneoka.

We immediately called the Japanese commanders and General Ando to a conference, which lasted for the rest of the morning. They impressed on us again that there was a strong element of extremism and lawlessness in Den Pasar, although at present it was latent and ill-armed. With some indignation I asked why, if they knew of it, they had taken no steps to suppress it; they replied uneasily that they had been without instructions, which indeed seemed to be true. They could tell us little of the situation outside Den Pasar, but believed that there were a few small bands in the countryside, especially in the west, who were supplied with arms by sea from Java; although they had established an effective blockade of the ports they could not hope, with their limited forces, to control the entire western coastline. Indeed, as I

---

[1] By the term 'extremists' I mean the Javanese-controlled, terrorist, independence movement which had as its object the removal of all Dutch and Allied control in the islands of Indonesia; despite the difference in religion and the mutual antipathy between the two peoples this movement had active supporters in Bali, particularly among the youth. They were also known as *Pemudas*, from the Malay word meaning 'youth'.

signalled General Mansergh, it was impossible to prevent the shipment of arms and agents from Java when the Bali Strait was only two miles wide.

As they were about to leave, Okuyama said to me, 'If the troops who follow you are British you need have no fear of trouble. But if they should be Dutch, then there may be incidents—although even then it would only be a few snipers.'

Refusing to be drawn by this obvious bait I answered that I knew nothing of the composition of the main force, but that in any event I expected his troops to see that there were no incidents. However, I sent a signal to Colonel Ter Meulen warning him of the danger and asking him to take precautions on D Day to ensure that one or two isolated shots should not develop into a major engagement.

Speaking neither Malay nor Balinese,[1] I badly needed an interpreter, and so I asked for Miura, whose Malay was as good as his English, to be attached to my staff. In addition, the Japanese gave me a chauffeur-mechanic to maintain our three staff cars. His name was Shimada, a simple, smiling lad of twenty-two who came from Yokohama and had been a merchant seaman before the war. He was a competent mechanic though an erratic driver, and he was a useful interpreter too, for he had a smattering of English and a good deal of Malay. He was a genial, carefree fellow with a perpetual grin on his ugly little pock-marked face; but he was a tireless and willing worker and, as we soon discovered, he had plenty of courage.

In the afternoon Neville went to inspect the beaches and Shaw drove to Kuta to examine the airfield. I made Miura take me to the prison where the Japanese were holding the headmen who had led the revolt of 13th December. My instructions gave me no authority to order their release, and if, as the Japanese maintained, they were dangerous terrorists, they were better in custody; but at least I could ensure that they were decently treated.

That evening Shaw and I drove the five miles to Sanoer to pay our respects to the famous Adrien Le Mayeur. He was a painter well known in south-east Asia, whose fame had already penetrated to Europe before the war. He had lived and worked in Bali for many years, and had built and furnished his own house; it stood on the beach, looking east across the lagoon to the line of white breakers on the coral reef that encircled those smooth

---

[1] There are three Balinese languages—high, low and middle, the last being a hybrid of the first two. High and low Balinese are not different dialects but separate languages, yet every Balinese must know both. For their rigid caste system dictates that, to take an example, a peasant addressing a rajah must speak to him in high Balinese, but the rajah would reply to him in low Balinese. Low Balinese is the native language of the island, whereas high Balinese is of Javanese or Sanskrit origin. Malay, which is the Hindustani of the Archipelago, is understood in Bali but is not spoken by the people amongst themselves.

and shallow waters and kept them clear of shark and barracuda. We had heard also of his beautiful Balinese wife, Polok, in her childhood a famous Legong dancer and afterwards the model for many of his best paintings.

Leaving the car at the end of the track we walked across the soft, shell-strewn sand past the white hulls of the fishing boats, carved in the shape of the mythical 'elephant fish' with eyes painted in their prows to enable them to see in the dark; through the fringe of palms and undergrowth on our right filtered the rays of the setting sun, etching rivulets of gold on the calm surface of the lagoon. Out of the silence ahead there appeared two figures plodding towards us: a slight, emaciated man whose age I judged to be near seventy, wearing only an old pair of shorts and sandals, and a tall, well-built, even husky girl with a golden skin and an expression of singular sweetness and serenity. She was wearing a magenta skirt with a green silk sash and a deep blue, gold-embroidered breast cloth.

'Le Mayeur,' the man introduced himself in a thin, reedy voice. 'Allow me to present my wife, Polok. We are very pleased to welcome you to our home.'

The house was built in Balinese style, of palm wood and bamboo, with a well-thatched roof of grass. There were no outside walls to the rooms; they were left open to the cooling breezes, the soft night scents and the murmur of the breakers on the reef. All the furniture was of bamboo. The house was filled with a profusion of Balinese carvings in wood and stone—gods and demons, animals and men; two squat stone demons with scarlet hibiscus flowers in their ears stood guard upon the porch. The walls were hung with Le Mayeur's paintings, most of them portraits of Polok and her friends. A cool and spacious living-room gave on to a veranda which overlooked a long, narrow compound enclosed by thorn hedges and bright with scarlet and yellow hibiscus and canna lilies; nearby stood a simple open summer house with a raised matting floor, where Le Mayeur and his guests usually took their meals.

While we sat talking on the veranda in the last of the daylight, Polok's two handsome maidservants brought us *arak* and small dishes of rice and meat with it.

'I hope you will come often,' said Polok in her halting, sing-song English. 'You can bathe and then eat with us. I will make you the special Balinese *bébé guling*.'[1]

We asked Le Mayeur how he had fared under the Japanese occupation.

'It was very worrying, of course,' he told us, 'but not really bad. At first they were very strict, but afterwards they left us alone. In the beginning, when the Dutch went away, the Balinese came and robbed my house; they took away many of my things, even the furniture, but later on I got some of them

---

[1] Roast sucking pig and rice.

back. They are great thieves, the Balinese,' he laughed, 'but they are like children, not really vicious.'

'Are we going to have a lot of trouble here, do you think?'

'Trouble? Yes, you can have some trouble. The Japanese of course were not popular, but they excited the people against you; and now that they see what is happening in Java some of the young men have big ideas and want to get rid of all foreigners. However, the older people are more sensible and want things to go slowly, and if you are firm with the troublemakers you will have their support.'

In the week that followed, whenever our work permitted, we would drive to Sanoer about seven in the morning, bathe in the lagoon and breakfast afterwards with the Le Mayeurs. Their knowledge of the district and people around Den Pasar was of the greatest help to us in those early days; and our affection grew daily for this kindly, easy-going couple and their two servants whom they regarded as part of their family.

One day, after a lunch of Polok's *bébé guling*, we sat on the veranda and listened to a *gamelan*[1] of musicians invited by Le Mayeur to play us Balinese music. The orchestra of some twenty young men squatted beside their instruments, forming a hollow square in the compound; the instruments were all percussion, which the musicians struck with light mallets. There were metallophones with polished bronze keys of different pitch; heavy gongs to play deep notes; two sets of twelve and ten bells each, arranged in a wooden frame; a pair of drums—a large 'male' and smaller 'female'—wrapped in chequered black and white cloth to shield them from evil vibrations; sets of cymbals, and bells, metal tubes and a small, light gong held in the lap and beaten with a stick.

The music was unlike any I had heard either in Europe or the East. Above the distant sound of the breakers on the reef it beat upon our ears—the pure, ringing notes of the metallophones, the soft, sweet chimes of the bells, the deep, mellow boom of the gongs, all superbly controlled by the throbbing pulse of the double-headed drums; now a gentle, soothing melody, now a wild, fast, exultant rhythm, the notes came to us like drops of clearest water through the still and heavy air.

Later we persuaded Polok, not without difficulty, to show us some of the movements of the *Legong*. She explained that this, the finest of Balinese dances,[2] must be performed by young, unmarried girls and so it was a long

---

[1] The orchestra of Bali and Java. The Balinese, strangely enough, have no written music.

[2] But it does not seem to be among the most ancient. For a full account of this dance and its origins see *Island of Bali* by Miguel Covarrubias, Cassell, 1937, pp. 224-30, and *Dance and Drama in Bali* by Beryl de Zoete and Walter Spies, Faber & Faber,

time since she had been able to dance it; moreover, it properly required three girls—two principals, the *legongs*, and their attendant, the *tjondong*. However, she wrapped herself in the heavy, tightly constricting, gold and crimson brocade garments of a *legong*, fastened on her head a golden diadem interwoven with fresh frangipani blossoms and, clasping a small fan in her right hand, stepped on to the floor.

Legong has been described as 'the flower of bodily movement at its utmost intensity of vibration.'[1] Although, as she said, Polok could give us no more than a bare idea of what it should be, the grace and vitality of her movements held us entranced. Now she stood poised with knees flexed, stamping her foot at each accent of the music, the vibrations spreading to her thigh, up her whole body and even to her neck, shaking the flowers in her hair; now she glided across the floor, one arm outstretched with the fingers tense and quivering. Her face was expressionless, even melancholy; but her eyes, darting from side to side in quick, sudden flashes, and her long, fluttering fingers gave life and warmth to this symphony of movement, colour and sound. The tense, absorbed faces of the musicians glistened in the afternoon sunlight, which flooded the flowering garden in a blaze of green and yellow and scarlet; between the notes of the orchestra we heard the fainter, unceasing music of the surf.

From the moment of our arrival our house became the centre of interest for the population of Den Pasar, especially for the women and children. From early morning until dusk there was a crowd gathered around our gates: handsome, bronze young men strolling up and down, hand in hand;[2] children staring wide-eyed and solemn or grinning shyly, then turning away or hiding their faces in sudden embarrassment; old women squatting on their haunches chewing betel nut and spitting streams of the scarlet juice on to the ground; golden, bare-breasted girls with baskets of fruit, walking with rippling muscles and superb, erect carriage and smiling lazily and seductively at the smart young sentries. The latter, without concealing their appreciation of the beautiful bare flesh exposed to them at such close quarters, contrived to preserve a soldierly decorum in the face of temptation; the signallers, true to their independent tradition, affected a cynical indifference and deplored the absence of a cinema.

1938, pp. 218-32. The dance tells a story, or variations of a story, from ancient Javanese legend.

[1] *Dance and Drama in Bali*, p. 218.

[2] In Bali this is a usual practice and is not considered in the lease effeminate.

VII

BALI AND THE BALINESE

To give an adequate picture of the island and people of Bali is beyond the scope of this work or the ingenuity of its author. The infinite variety of Balinese life, religion and culture has exhausted volumes of literature on art and anthropology with which I have not the knowledge, the skill or the impudence to compete.[1] A very brief outline is all I can attempt.

Lying between eight and nine degrees south of the Equator Bali naturally enjoys a warm climate and an even temperature throughout the year; there is in fact less than ten degrees variation between the warmest and coolest months. Sea winds preserve the island from the burning heat of other equatorial lands, but from November until April the north-west monsoons bring heavy rainfall and the discomforts of a high humidity; the pleasantest months are from June to September, when a cool, dry wind blows from Australia.

The island is mountainous, with high volcanic peaks on the north, east and west; the highest of them, the great volcano Gunung Agung, which rises over ten thousand feet, is sacred to all Balinese, who regard it as the navel (*puséh*) of the world. In the south the foothills drop gradually to the sea, intersected by steep, wooded ravines and watercourses; the slopes are terraced with superb skill in tier after tier of *sawas*, or small paddy-fields, that produce each year two crops of the finest rice in South-East Asia. The north-western corner of the island, which unfortunately I was never able to visit, is very little populated because of the lack of running water; there are found tiger, wild boar and giant lizards, which exist nowhere else on Bali. Elephants, incidentally, have never existed on Bali, and their appearance in Balinese art is due to Indian and Javanese influence. The average density of population over the whole island is 1,000 per square mile, but in the Gianjar district of South Bali it is 2,300, making a total of a million and a half inhabitants.

To the Balinese the mountain-tops are the homes of the gods and of the spirits of their ancestors, whom they worship and who descend to earth on feast days; the sea is the haunt of evil spirits and demons. The land between

---

[1] Foremost among works in the English language I would commend to readers, Miguel Covarrubias's valuable and informative *Island of Bali* and the more technical study, *Dance and Drama in Bali* by Beryl de Zoete and Walter Spies. John Coast's *Dancing out of Bali*, Faber & Faber, 1954, gives a fascinating account of more recent conditions on the island.

is, to them, the whole world. They recognize, of course, that other countries exist, but those countries mean nothing to them, and they regard their inhabitants as unfortunates whose past or present imperfections have rendered them unfit to live in Bali; exile for a Balinese is far worse than death, and Miss Emily Hahn records an ordinance of the old Dutch East India Company forbidding the importation of Balinese slaves into Java because they so often ran amok.[1]

In their fear and hatred of the sea the Balinese are exceptional among island peoples. At Sanoer I saw men wading in the lagoon a few yards off shore with casting nets, or putting to sea in canoes with triangular sails and curiously carved and painted prows, to hunt the sea turtles that are a favourite delicacy at banquets; but most Balinese avoid even the coast and the beaches. In the words of Covarrubias 'they are one of the rare island peoples in the world who turn their eyes not outward to the waters, but upward to the mountain tops.'[2]

Here it is perhaps worthwhile quoting Covarrubias again on another peculiarity of the Balinese—their attitude to death, or rather to the ceremony of cremation. 'It is in their cremation ceremonies,' he writes, 'that the Balinese have their greatest fun. A cremation is an occasion for gaiety and not for mourning, since it represents the accomplishment of their most sacred duty: the ceremonial burning of the corpses of the dead to liberate their souls so that they can thus attain the higher worlds and be free for reincarnation into better things.'[3]

Although a strange, even a unique people, the Balinese are not a pure race; they are a mixture of the ancient Indonesian inhabitants of the islands with Hindu-Javanese, Chinese and Indian colonists. Hindu dynasties flourished in the Archipelago from the seventh to the fifteenth or early sixteenth centuries, the most famous of them being the Srivijaya in Sumatra and the Madjapahit in Java. For much of this period Bali was under the rule of Hindu-Javanese kings. On the collapse of the Madjapahit dynasty about the end of the fifteenth century, under the pressure of Islamic penetration, the surviving Hindu-Javanese aristocracy of priests and warriors migrated to Bali, where they established their rule and their culture. The son of the last Madjapahit ruler styled himself *Dewa Agung*[4] or supreme ruler of Bali, and divided the island into principalities to which he appointed rajahs. These principalities gradually developed into independent kingdoms, though theoretically

---

[1] *Raffles of Singapore*, Alder, 1948. On the other hand, the Balinese conquered Lombok in 1740 and established a prosperous colony there, ruled by a rajah.

[2] Covarrubias, op. cit., p. 10.

[3] Ibid, p. 359.

[4] Literally 'Divine Great'. When I was in Bali this was still the title of the Rajah of Klungkung, the paramount rajah of the island.

acknowledging the supremacy of the *Dewa Agung* before the arrival of the Dutch they were perpetually at war among themselves.

'It was of extreme significance for the cultural development of Bali that in the exodus of the rulers, the priests, and the intellectuals of what was the most civilized race of the Eastern islands, the cream of Javanese culture was transplanted as a unit into Bali. There the art, the religion and philosophy of the Hindu-Javanese were preserved and have flourished practically undisturbed until today. When the fury of intolerant Islamism drove the intellectuals of Java into Bali, they brought with them their classics and continued to cultivate their poetry and art, so that when Sir Stamford Raffles wanted to write the history of Java, he had to turn to Bali for what remains of the once great literature of Java.'[1]

The Hindu-Javanese princes established a feudal, often vicious and oppressive dominion over the native Balinese; they claimed and tried to enforce absolute power over the persons of their subjects. The Dutchman Dr. Julius Jacobs, who visited South Bali in the early 1880's, mentions a particularly savage example.[2] Every adult male Balinese, he says, was obliged to contribute a tax to his rajah in the form of work; if a man died without leaving a son old enough to take over this work, his widow and female children became the rajah's property. Old women were employed in the palace, the middle-aged put to heavy manual labour; but the young girls— often before the age of puberty—were forced to become prostitutes and pay as much as nine-tenths of their earnings to the rajah. In Badung, the old principality of Den Pasar, Dr. Jacobs met several of these prostitutes under the age of puberty. Each rajah owned between two and three hundred of these unfortunate girls—a considerable source of income.

Nevertheless, the Balinese, in their self-governing village communities, were often able to mitigate the oppression of their rulers by the threat of boycott and passive resistance. Moreover, in the mountains there are still a few villages of pure descendants of the ancient Indonesian inhabitants, who live in strict isolation and have protected the purity of their stock by the most rigid taboos against marriage outside the community; the most interesting and the most exclusive is the village of Tenganan near Karangasem in East Bali. These people, who style themselves Bali Aga, or 'original Balinese', have never accepted the Hinduism of the Javanese invaders, but cling with fanatical devotion to their ancient traditions and beliefs. The Hindu-Balinese aristocracy seem to have respected them and left them alone.

---

[1] Covarrubias, op. cit., p. 28.

[2] *Eenigen Tijd onder de Baliërs*, Batavia, 1883, a most fascinating work unfortunately not published in English; for the translations quoted here I am indebted to my friend Daan Hubrecht.

The statement that the Balinese are Hindus requires considerable qualification. It is impossible to give here a satisfactory account of Balinese religious belief and custom; but the Balinese seem to have absorbed a little from each of the sects and cults that reached their island, adapted the new teachings to suit their own habits and ideas, and superimposed them on their own primitive animistic religion. Indeed, 'it is not unlikely,' says Covarrubias,[1] 'that in the future "Sanghyang Widi", the exalted name that the missionaries have adopted for Jesus, will become a first cousin of Siva and Buddha and will enjoy offerings and a shrine where he can rest when he chooses to visit Bali.'[2]

Of far more religious importance to the Balinese than the imported Hinduism of their conquerors are their own traditional rites connected with the worship of their ancestors' spirits; of the gods of fertility; of the gods of fire and water, earth and sun; of the mountains—the two great volcanoes, Batur and Gunung Agung, have their shrines in every village temple—and of other lesser gods and demons. This worship, as Covarrubias points out, is The backbone of the Balinese religion, which is generally referred to as Hinduism, but which is in reality too close to the earth, too animistic, to be taken as the same esoteric religion as that of the Hindus of India. ... It is true that Hindu gods and practices are constantly in evidence, but their aspect and significance differ in Bali to such an extent from orthodox Hinduism *that we find the primitive beliefs of a people who never lost contact with the soil rising supreme over the religious philosophy and practices of their masters.* . . . Religion is to the Balinese both race and nationality. . . . The religious sages, the Brahmanic priests, remain outsiders, aloof from the ordinary Balinese, who have their own priests, simple people whose office is to guard and sweep the community temples, in which there are no idols, no images of gods to be worshipped. The temples are frequented by the ancestral gods. . . . *The Balinese live with their forefathers in a great family of the dead and the living.* . . . *The religion of Bali is a set of rules of behaviour, a mode of life.*[3]

When, therefore, the Balinese speak of their gods they do not mean the gods of orthodox Hinduism—indeed, the only Hindu god actually worshipped in Balinese temples is Surya, the Sun, who has somehow achieved the dignity of head of the Balinese pantheon; they mean a wide variety of protective spirits, all of them connected in some way with the cult of ancestry. Into this family they have also absorbed certain characters from Hindu mythology to whom they have taken a fancy. However, I might

---

[1] Covarrubias, op. cit., p. 263.

[2] It is not true, as is sometimes asserted, that the Dutch excluded missionaries; it was the religious outlook of the Balinese that proved unresponsive to missionary zeal.

[3] Covarrubias, op. cit., p. 260-1. (My italics.)

mention that when I questioned the Swiss artist Theo Meier on the number and variety of Balinese deities, he laughed.

'There are only two gods in Bali—*takut* and *malu*! Those two rule the lives of all Balinese; the old rajahs ruled through them, and you will find you must do so too.'

Takut means fear; *malu* is shame, embarrassment or 'face'. Of the power of *takut* over the Balinese we were to have immediate and almost daily experience.

Like the Manichaeans the Balinese believe that there is perpetual war between the equally powerful forces of good and evil; between their gods and protecting spirits on the one hand, and on the other the demons and *leyaks*, or witches, whose purpose and joy it is to destroy humanity. It is necessary to propitiate both to avoid arousing the wrath of either. On its ability to preserve a proper balance between the two depends the physical and spiritual health of each community and family. Certain acts or conditions of individual members can make the whole community *sebel*, or unclean, and therefore vulnerable to evil forces. Such acts extend beyond the unpardonable crimes of suicide, bestiality, incest and the desecration of a temple, to quite innocent or unavoidable breaches of taboo; a menstruating woman, for instance, is *sebel* and must be secluded, and parents who have twins will render their village *sebel*. To such a people, in the words of Mr. Raymond Mortimer, 'sin is not a disregard for conscience but a breaking, no matter how unintentional, of a taboo; and the resulting pollution can be removed only by ritual cleansings and sacrifice.'[1]

The Hindu caste system, which is an essential feature of Balinese society, was not established in its present form until the middle of the fourteenth century, when Bali was overrun by a famous Madjapahit general, Gadja Mada. Previously the old Balinese aristocracy had their own caste system, which still survives among the Bali Aga.

There are four main castes, of which more than ninety per cent of Balinese belong to the lowest, the Sudras. The three noble castes are the Brahmanas, the priests; the Satrias, the princes, and the Wesias, the warrior caste. All three claim divine origin—from Brahma, the Creator—which is probably why the common people hold them in such respect. The Brahmanas are theoretically the highest, although the Satrias are inclined to contest their superiority; their influence is religious rather than political, but they serve as judges in the courts; their own laws forbid them to engage in commerce. Brahmana men carry the title *Ida Bagus*, and the women are styled *Ida Ayu*, both meaning 'Eminent and Beautiful'. The two principal titles of the Satrias are *Anak Agung*, 'Child of the Great', and *Tjokorde*, Prince. Most of the nobility,

---

[1] Review in the *Sunday Times* of 7th September 1958.

however, belong to the Wesias and carry the title, *Gusti*; they have considerable political influence.[1]

There do not seem to be any 'untouchables', as in India, but certain professions are 'unclean' and will pollute a village if practised within its boundaries; among them are, strangely enough, pottery, indigo-dying and the manufacture of arak—a powerful, fiery spirit distilled from the juice of the sugar palm.

An important survival from the pre-Hindu castes are the pandés, or blacksmiths, descendants of the ancient fire priests, who worship the volcano Batur. They enjoy great respect among all Balinese because they have the magical powers to handle with impunity the holy elements of fire and iron; even a Brahmana must address a pandé in high Balinese. The pandés make the magic krises, symbols of a family's virility; a man will invest much of his fortune in his kris and the jewellery decorating it, for the richness of his kris determines his economic status.[2]

While it is untrue to say that the Balinese are 'caste-ridden', they are intensely—and proudly—caste-conscious. Relations between the castes are distinguished by an elasticity and friendliness unknown in India, but the Balinese pay careful attention to caste etiquette and to the rank conferred upon a man by his birth; this respect for rank, strange among so easy-going a people, is as much a matter of good manners as of duty. When strangers meet upon the road the first question they ask each other is 'What is your caste?' Thereafter the higher caste will continue the conversation in low Balinese, and the lower caste will reply to him in high. It is unthinkable for a man of low caste to place himself at a higher level in a room than someone of higher caste. For example, a Sudra would never stand upright in the presence of a seated Brahmana or Satria, but would immediately sit down at a lower level, probably on the floor; and the common people—who are not ashamed to think of themselves as such—would always bow their heads when passing a nobleman. I remember an occasion when I was staying in the house of the Swiss painter, Theo Meier, and a Brahmana came to visit him; as soon as the visitor was seated Meier signed to me to sit down. 'You see' he explained to me later, 'it would have been the insult for you to have remained standing. You would have made yourself higher than the *Ida Bagus*.'

Only the laws of marriage are inflexible between the castes. A man may marry a woman of an equal or lower caste, but never may a woman marry a

---

[1] For example, a famous Balinese terrorist and hero, killed in battle with the Dutch soon after I left, was Gusti Ngurah Rai; Ngurah is a title assumed by some nobility to indicate the purity of their descent.

[2] Covarrubias, op. cit., p. 199. When a rajah marries a girl of low caste she is often married ceremonially to his Kris, the prince not attending the ceremony.

man of lower caste; even sexual intercourse between the two is forbidden, and in former times was punishable by the death of the guilty pair.

The life of the Balinese is concentrated in their villages. Each village is a small, independent republic with its own council of Elders and officials who are elected by the community, who are generally unpaid, and who govern as representatives of the ancestral spirits; all villagers have equal rights and obligations. Each *desa*, as these independent villages are called, will have three temples: the civil temple, or *pura desa*, where the Elders meet in council and where the main feasts take place; the 'temple of origin', or *pura puséh* the ancient village shrine, dedicated to the founder of the community; and the *pura dalem*, the temple of the dead, outside the village in the cemetery. Balinese cemeteries are desolate and forbidding spots, shunned by the people, especially after dark when they are haunts of the abominable *leyaks*; these malignant witches, under their terrible queen, Rangda—a hideous creature with lolling tongue, long fierce fangs and monstrous drooping breasts—bring plagues on the island and live off the blood and entrails of young or unborn children and the blood of pregnant women.

Usually a village consists of a number of family compounds, each containing several pavilions housing relatives or related families; every compound is surrounded by a low wall of whitewashed mud, pierced by a narrow thatched gateway with a raised doorstep. A wide avenue, shaded by great trees and flanked by deep irrigation ditches, runs through the centre of the village in the direction of the Balinese cardinal points—'from the mountain to the sea', or from north to south. They are a lovely sight, these villages, with their long, beautifully proportioned walls and thatched roofs half-hidden in cool, shady groves of banana trees, mangoes and tall, slim, plume-topped coco-palms.

The work of the village, in particular the cultivation of the rice-fields, is organized on a communal or co-operative basis; *subaks*, or village water boards, control the vitally important irrigation. Every villager who owns a ricefield is obliged to join the *subak* and to carry out its orders. 'The objectives of the *subak* are to give the small agriculturist the assurance that he will not lack water, to police the dams effectively so that strangers will not divert the water supply, to settle disputes, and to attend to the communal rice festivals. In the village the society assumes full social, technical, and administrative authority in all matters concerning irrigation and agriculture. Like other Balinese associations, the spirit of the *subak* is essentially communal; all members abide by the same rules, each one being allotted work in relation to the amount of water he receives. Certain stipulations are made to prevent individuals from holding more land than would be convenient to the community. A man 'who has more land than he can work is compelled to share the produce with people appointed to help him.'[1]

As I have said, the Balinese are primarily a nation of agriculturists whose standard of rice cultivation is the highest in the Far East. Rice itself is treated with extreme reverence and there is an elaborate religious ritual connected with all aspects of its cultivation; it must be handled with great respect, and must be collected from the granaries in silence and only in the daytime. Except in the north and west, where the soil is barren and water scarce, the whole island is intensively cultivated; people who live in those arid districts grow corn and sweet potatoes, which are considered inferior foods to rice. Only men may plant and attend to the rice, but women and children help with the harvest.

The rajahs had no voice in the councils of these self-governing village republics, although they appointed *pungawas* as provincial governors and tax-collectors; the *pungawa* was usually a relative of the rajah. 'Bali presents the amazing spectacle of a land where the deeply rooted agrarian communalism of the people has continued to exist side by side with the feudalism of the noble landlords.'[2]

The administration of justice is largely in the hands of the village councils; moral sanctions and the weight of public opinion are more effective than imprisonment or fine. The most terrible of all punishments for a Balinese is expulsion from the village, when the offender is publicly declared 'dead' to the community; when the Dutch abolished the death penalty this became the capital punishment. 'A man expelled from his village cannot be admitted into another community, so he becomes a total outcast—a punishment greater than physical death to the Balinese mind. It often happens that a man who has been publicly shamed kills himself.'[3]

Dutch relations with Bali date back to the end of the sixteenth century, when a fleet of their ships visited the ruler. The ill-famed Dutch East India Company engaged in trade—and political intrigue—in the island until its dissolution in 1798. In the mid-nineteenth century the Dutch Government obtained from the Balinese princes a vague recognition of its sovereignty; but it was not until 1882 that the Dutch, provoked by some stupid acts of Balinese pirates and 'wreckers' against their shipping, launched a military expedition against North Bali and occupied the states of Buleleng (Singaradja) and Djembrana. At the same time they concluded treaties with the rajahs of South Bali under which the rajahs renounced piracy and

---

[1] Covarrubias, op. cit., pp. 72, 73.
[2] Covarrubias, op. cit., p. 83.
[3] Covarrubias, op. cit., p. 64.

'wrecking', and promised to abolish slavery and *suttee*.[1] According to Dr. Jacobs, who visited South Bali shortly afterwards, the last two promises were not honoured.

During the following years the rulers of South Bali engaged in perpetual civil war; in 1900 the Dutch, appealed to for help by the local rajah, annexed the principality of Gianjar. In September 1906 they occupied Badung and Tabanan, and in 1908 they annexed the last independent state, Klungkung; these last three occupations were accompanied by the mass suicides of the rajahs, their chiefs, generals and the women of their households, who threw themselves with spears and krises against the bullets of the invading army.

The army continued in occupation until 1914, when a police force took over its duties. The Dutch placed the administration of the island in the hands of two Residents, one in Singaradja, the other in Den Pasar; but they continued to govern through the Council of Rajahs—the eight rulers of the old autonomous principalities—attaching to each Rajah a Controller as adviser, or rather supervisor. The village councils they left alone, contenting themselves with the appointment of their own *pungawas* in place of those of the Rajahs. This system continued until the Japanese occupation of 1942.

The physical beauty of the Balinese has been proverbial for hundreds of years, and at one time Balinese women were in great demand in the slave markets of the East and West Indies. This reputation, we soon discovered, was no myth; handsome looks, fine physique and dignified bearing are characteristic of both men and women. Nowhere in the world have I seen girls so perfect in the flawless texture of their golden-brown skins, their narrow waists, full, firm breasts, slender arms and delicate hands and feet; the men are small but lithe, quick but graceful in their movements, gentle in their manner yet alert and quivering with vitality; even the elderly retain their dignity of bearing and grace of movement.

'Childlike' is the label attached in this hideous age to a people unresponsive to the language of the demagogue, the high-pressure salesman and the advertising hound; it is a label that bears no resemblance to the character of the Balinese, although they prefer their traditional way of life to that of the modern world, which, they would certainly agree with Pierre Louÿs, '*succombe sous un envahissement de laideur.*'

They have neither the ignorance nor the innocence of childhood, although they give an impression of its simplicity. They are, as I have said, the most skilful agriculturists in Asia, they are painters, craftsmen, poets, musicians and dancers; and their art has aroused the envy of a civilization to whose arrogance, ugliness and brutality they are largely indifferent.

---

[1] The immolation of a nobleman's widows, concubines, and slaves on his funeral pyre. In Bali *suttee* was never compulsory; the victims of this grisly practice were volunteers, not only in theory but in fact.

They take little thought for the sufferings of animals, but they are indulgent to children and would never think of beating them, preferring to coax them into obedience as equals; on the other hand they do not pamper them but are inclined to leave them from their earliest years to the care of older children. In this way the young quickly acquire a sense of responsibility, self-confidence and poise seldom found before maturity in Anglo-Saxons.

They have a refreshingly bawdy sense of humour and a Rabelaisian turn of wit; women and even children are permitted to make jokes which in Europe would be received in shocked silence. There is no prudery in the Balinese, but behaviour between the sexes in public is characterized by extreme modesty; for example, although men and women frequently bathe naked in pools or rivers by the roadside, it would be the grossest bad manners for a man to look at a woman bathing, let alone to take photographs as tourists used to do.[1] They are resourceful, sensitive, intelligent, extremely courteous and usually good-humoured. Though naturally timid they have a fierce pride, and when roused are capable of excessive cruelty; of this darker side to their character I was to have some grim experience.

The Balinese pay careful attention to cleanliness and the care of their bodies. They bathe regularly every morning and evening and frequently during the day, scrubbing themselves with pumice stone to cleanse and stimulate the skin and remove the hair. The traditional everyday dress of both men and women is the simple *kamben*, a cloth skirt reaching from the hips to the feet on women, to the knees on men. In addition to the *kamben*, women wear a bright-coloured sash round the waist and a long scarf thrown over one shoulder or tied round the head to hold the hair in place; men wear a headcloth tied as a turban in different styles to suit the wearer's taste. Although the Balinese normally go bare above the waist, both men and women cover the breast in the company of superiors. Priests wear white, and a high priest or *pedanda* goes bareheaded and carries a staff surmounted by a crystal ball.

For temple feasts, weddings and other ceremonial occasions the Balinese dress much more elaborately, wrapping themselves in rich cloth and brocade from armpits to feet and adorning their hair with beautiful and scented flowers. Although it is customary for men to put flowers in their hair, over each ear, only a Satria may wear the scarlet hibiscus; infringement of this rule by a man of lower caste carried in former times severe penalties. According to Theo Meier the offender was tied to a post in the market-place while groups of old men stood in front of him spitting peppers into his eyes.

---

[1] I hear from a recent visitor that in the new airport building on Bali there is a prominent notice informing visitors that 'It is forbidden to photograph native women without breast coverings, whether on purpose or by accident.'

Women in North Bali wear a hideous garment called a *badju*, a tight-fitting and usually dirty cotton blouse originally forced upon them, I understand, by the Dutch authorities in the 1880's to lessen the temptation to their troops;[1] by the end of the last war, unfortunately, the fashion had begun to spread to the rest of the island. European dress has become increasingly popular since the war, especially among the young men, who consider a shirt and slacks or shorts much smarter than the *kamben*.

While there are fine artists among them, and their sculpture, particularly in wood, is famous, it is in music, dancing and the drama that the Balinese take their chief delight; every community has at least one orchestra—many have two or three—and a troop of dancers; the villages vie with each other in the excellence of their musicians and dancers, all of whom, of course, are unpaid. 'There is not *one* music in Bali,' writes Beryl de Zoete. 'There is an appropriate music for every occasion, and an appropriate type of *gamelan*: for birthdays, tooth filing [at puberty], weddings, cremations, for temple feasts and processions to the sea with the holy images, for purifications and the driving away of disease and demons. There is naturally also an appropriate music for every kind of dance. . . .'[2] According to Covarrubias the Balinese attribute a divine origin to music and dancing.[3]

Elaborate dramatic performances, shadow-plays, and opera, are regular features of every festival, every wedding, birthday and cremation; they often last the entire night. The themes are ancient legends, a favourite being the struggle between Rangda and her *leyaks*, and the *Barong*, a kind of giant pekinese who champions the people of Bali and tries to protect them from Rangda's plagues.[4]

The Balinese are also devoted to gambling and cockfighting, although the Dutch government used to restrict both. The cocks are carried to the meeting halls, where the fights are held, in curious round baskets of coconut leaves which have handles and are woven round the bird's body, leaving the tail outside. For the fight the spur on the right foot is removed and replaced by a wicked steel blade five or six inches long, with a needle-sharp point; this practice, of course, shortens the fight, which is to the death. When a cock is wounded its owner will often revive it by massage and by blowing his own breath into its lungs.[5] The enthusiasm of the Balinese for this sport is as

---

[1] Covarrubias, op. cit., p. 111.

[2] Dance and Drama in Bali, pp. 6 and 7.

[3] Covarrubias, op. cit., p. 216.

[4] It is obviously beyond the scope of this book to attempt any description of the various fascinating plays and dances of Bali; for a concise account see Covarrubias, op. cit. pp. 205-55, and for a full study I recommend *Dance and Drama in Bali* by Beryl de Zoete and Walter Spies.

[5] Covarrubias, op. cit., p. 114.

intense as that of the British for football or the Spanish for bulls; in ancient times, indeed, men would sometimes gamble away their whole fortunes in cockfights, even staking their wives and children. It was for this reason that the Dutch government intervened.

It is only too easy to fall in love with Bali and to blind oneself to the vices which, though not immediately apparent, are an essential part of the people's character. Only the cantankerous Dr. Julius Jacobs, who visited the rajahs of South Bali in a semi-official capacity, seems to have had no difficulty in penetrating the veneer of Balinese charm; indeed he finds a sour satisfaction in exposing their faults. Contrary to the general impression of authors, he says, who represent the Balinese as patient, hard-working and courageous, he found them extremely egotistical, effeminate, cowardly, cynical, revengeful and jealous; a Balinese, according to him, has no feeling for the sufferings of others, and will undertake nothing that does not hold out some profit for himself. But he does admit that the women have unusual charm, and that they accept with loyalty and without complaint the selfish and callous ill-treatment of their menfolk.

Between these two extreme opinions—that of Covarrubias and that of Dr. Jacobs—I confess I find it difficult to judge; certainly there is an element of truth in both, and, though the picture I shall always cherish is nearer to Covarrubias's than to Jacobs's, I came myself into unpleasantly close contact with the seamy side of the Balinese character. Of their jealousy and cruelty the story of the dancer Sampih is a terrible but typical example.

In the autumn of 1952, when the Javanese Central Government were in control of Bali, Sampih left the island with a troupe of dancers organized by John Coast to tour Europe and America; they met with resounding success, and their star was Sampih. At the end of the tour he returned to Bali to enjoy, as he no doubt thought, the envious adulation of his people. The envy he experienced all too soon. At the end of February 1954, he disappeared, and it was three days before his remains were found in a river bed; his jealous fellow-countrymen had cut his throat, chopped his body into pieces and thrown them in the river.[1]

To return to the brighter side, the Balinese have a passion for clubs; even more than the British the men are 'clubbable', although their women resent it less. There are *sekehe*, as they are called, for every conceivable purpose, some more frivolous in our eyes—though not to the Balinese—than others. Thus there are *sekehe* for fire-lighting and for hunting squirrels, who eat the coconuts; and there are *sekehe* for drinking *tuak*, and for sitting on bridges on Sunday mornings. Meetings are regular and a member who fails to turn up pays a fine in money or in kind. There are no mixed or ladies' *sekehe*.

---

[1] The story is told in John Coast's Dancing Out of Bali, p. 227.

The little grey squirrels that infest the coconut plantations are a serious nuisance to the villagers, causing devastation to the crop; the method of hunting them is a primitive stratagem with echoes of the brain-washing techniques of today. Armed with sticks and tin cans the members of the *sekehe* surround a plantation; gradually they close in, beating the tin cans with their sticks and making as much noise as they can. The squirrels, alarmed by the din, hop from tree-top to tree-top in panic. As the circle narrows, the squirrels become so nervous that they lose their footholds and fall to the ground, where they are quickly dispatched by the sticks of the villagers.

Tuak drinking is a favourite pastime of the elderly men.[1] *Tuak*, or toddy, is brewed from the juice of the sugar palm; it looks and tastes somewhat like farm cider and, though not so intoxicating, makes a most refreshing and mellowing drink. It should be drunk within forty-eight hours of being tapped, for it soon turns to vinegar; and so when people talk of 'old' or 'young' tuak they mean a difference only of a few hours. The *tuak*-drinking *sekehe* gather every evening before sundown; a member who fails to appear for a meeting must bring an extra 'bamboo' of tuak the next time—in fact he buys a round. The popularity of these clubs was the reason I found it so hard to get good tuak in the island. In Den Pasar I used to have a posse of small boys and girls scouting for me to find a good brew; when I passed in the street they would call out to me: '*Tabé* (hallo), *Tuan Tuak!*'

The Balinese begin their love life early, in fact they seldom delay it long after puberty. The attitude of the Sudras towards virginity is as 'progressive' as that of our most advanced Western civilizations; neither by law nor by custom is there an 'age of consent', the generally accepted principle being, in the words of the old west-country proverb, 'if they're big enough they're old enough'.

For example, it is not customary to say of a girl, 'She is still a virgin'; rather they say, after her first menstruation, 'she is *already* a virgin'—implying that she is unlikely to remain one.[2] Widows, therefore, and divorced women have no difficulty in remarrying; but adultery, especially by a woman, is a serious offence in their eyes, and used to be punished by death.[3]

Every Balinese considers it one of his first duties to marry and raise a family of sons to perpetuate his line and do honour to his spirit after his death. Men usually marry at eighteen, girls at sixteen, but since in those latitudes they mature at a much earlier age it is usual for both to have love

---

[1] In general the Balinese are moderate drinkers; I only met one who wasn't—a priest. Incidentally, the consumption of opium, very heavy in Dr. Jacobs' time, had almost disappeared in mine.

[2] The Bali Aga, on the other hand, consider that sexual intercourse carries pollution, and do not encourage it before marriage.

[3] Infidelity by the husband seems to be taken for granted.

affairs before; the idea of platonic love is foreign to the Balinese, who prefer to consummate their desire by sleeping together. In public, however, lovers behave with extreme discretion and decorum.

According to Dr. Jacobs,[1] who appears to have considered them as little better than sex maniacs, the Balinese are addicted to every conceivable form of sexual aberration; certainly in their paintings and temple reliefs they show some ingenious variations of the normal positions for intercourse. Much of what the doctor says on the subject is irrelevant to this work, impossible of verification by this author, and, even in the present state of the law risky to print. But he states categorically—in contrast to the opinion of Covarrubias[2]—that male and female homosexuality and Onanism were prevalent; he concludes with a sniff of disgust, 'cucumbers and bananas are used by Balinese girls not only as food'.

A couple will often live together before their wedding in a legal form of trial marriage known as *gendak*; the laws governing it protect the girl against desertion by her husband and legitimize children born during this period. The most usual form of marriage, however, is elopement or the more spectacular kidnapping of the bride by her suitor and his friends. The girl, though not of course her parents, is a party to the plot; she arranges to have her belongings taken secretly to her new home, and plans with her future husband the place—usually on the road or in the fields—where he and his friends will waylay her. She usually puts up the pretence of a fight, and any of her relatives who happen to be with her at the time are expected to try to prevent her abduction; but no other witnesses would dream of interfering, even to the extent of informing the girl's parents.

As soon afterwards as possible representatives of the husband will call upon the girl's outraged parents—they must pretend to be outraged even if they really approve of the marriage—to obtain their formal consent and fix the price the father will receive for his daughter. But a man who kidnaps a girl by force and against her will is liable to severe penalties, unless she chooses to remain with him.

The marriage is made binding in the sight of the gods by certain offerings which await the runaway couple at their new home; and it is an important point of law that the pair must consummate the wedding there before the offerings have wilted.[3] A public ceremony and feast usually follow a few weeks later. After marriage a girl leaves her own ancestral gods and worships her husband's.

In families of the higher castes a formal betrothal is more usual, often arranged by the parents. To the aristocracy a bride's virginity is important,

---

[1] Jacobs, op. cit., pp. 134-5.
[2] Covarrubias, op. cit., p. 145.
[3] Covarrubias, op. cit., p. 148.

and in old-fashioned weddings there is a barbaric ceremony in which the husband announces the defloration of his bride to the assembled guests while her women attendants verify the evidence.[1] Until recent times a rajah might order a subject to reserve him his daughter when she came of age; but children, though they may be betrothed very young, never marry before puberty.

Among the peasantry, though not among the aristocracy, women enjoy a degree of freedom unusual in Eastern countries; their rights are well defined and recognized by law and custom. They have the right to dispose of their own income and property without the consent or even the knowledge of their husbands; they manage the family finances and often contribute to them; nearly all the marketing is controlled by women. Moreover, unlike the Common Law of England, Balinese law does not hold a husband responsible for his wife's debts.

There are strict rules defining the work and duties of each sex. 'All heavy work requiring manly attributes—agriculture, building in wood or thatch, the care of cattle—as well as most of the trades and crafts ... is the work of men. Women own, raise, and sell chickens and pigs, but only men care for cows, buffaloes, and ducks.'[2] Similarly, the cooking of everyday meals is the task of women; but it is the privilege of men to prepare the food at the great banquets that mark all Balinese festivals. In the home women usually prefer to eat after their men have finished; but this does not imply any inferiority in their status.

Such, then, is the complicated, alluring and unpredictable race which, with no experience or qualifications and with none of the knowledge I have just recorded, I was called upon to govern.

---

[1] Covarrubias, op. cit., pp. 150-51.
[2] Covarrubias, op, cit., pp. 81-82.

VIII

TERRORISTS

The slight brown figure in the creased white linen suit shifted uncomfortably in his chair; his fingers, interlocked on his lap, twisted in an agony of nervousness and indecision while his flickering, frightened eyes, heavily pouched with fatigue and strain, darted round the veranda of his house, resting fearfully now on the compound at the back, now on the road and the front gate, where a pair of Buffs stood on guard. The Tjokorde Gdé Rake Sukawati was not ashamed to admit that he was badly scared; he had, it seemed, good reason.

A trusted friend of the Dutch and a most able statesman who by his education and rank enjoyed considerable influence and respect around Den Pasar, Sukawati was the first local dignitary with whom I had tried to make contact; I had lost no time in sending a message to his house, which was not far from my own headquarters, asking him to call on me. My messenger returned with a letter from the Tjokorde welcoming me to Bali, assuring me of his warmest sentiments but regretting that he dared not visit me in person. Taking a small escort I hastened to call on him myself.

Placing my men in positions where they could command all approaches to the house, I climbed a flight of steps to the open wooden veranda which ran round the outside. The Tjokorde received me alone, the few servants who had been with him vanishing at my approach; there was no doubt that my visit was causing him acute embarrassment and alarm. He spoke very softly, little above a whisper, trying to keep the tremor out of his voice.

'Forgive me, colonel, that I do not appear more hospitable. You do not know how dangerous is my situation. I am friendly to the Allies, and the leaders of the *Sukerela*—the terrorists—they know this. Once already they have taken me away—yes, kidnapped me from my own house! They did not kill me then, for I have many friends among the people; but others that they took have been killed or have disappeared. They kept me for two weeks, and when they let me go they warned me to have nothing to do with the Allies when they should come. Then, when you arrived three days ago, they threatened me again. Colonel, this time they will kill me. I am sorry I cannot help you. I am afraid.'

It was obviously difficult for me to reassure him; I knew too well the power of determined terrorism. As it was, he probably owed his life only to his popularity and to the terrorists' reluctance to outrage public opinion by the murder of a Satria. Others apparently had been less fortunate. But even if I could no longer expect him to help me, I must still protect him as a friend of the Dutch and a valuable ally in the future.

'I am going to put a guard on your house,' I told him, 'both by day and night—sentries at the back and the front; they will have orders to shoot on sight anyone trying to break in here. When you want to leave the house please let me know, and I will provide you with an escort.'

'What guards can you give me?'

'By day a pair of British soldiers and a pair of Japanese; by night a section of Japanese. Is that sufficient?'

'Can you trust the Japanese?'

I smiled. 'At this moment they are only too anxious to do all they can to help me.'

He seemed a little relieved and went on to tell me something of the situation around Den Pasar. In general, he said, the people were well-disposed towards us—this much I must have gathered from my reception among them in the last three days. But there was a small, well-organized body of extremists, many of them Javanese, who by murder and kidnapping had so terrorized the district that nobody would dare to collaborate with me openly; let me deal promptly and firmly with them, and he was sure that people would hasten to me with offers of help.

I asked if he would give me the names of the leading terrorists After some persuasion he gave me a few, fearfully and in a whisper, and told me the places where I might search for them. As I rose to go he spoke in a more earnest and resolute voice than he had used before:

'Believe me, you have many friends in this island. The people are sick of the Japanese—when they heard you had arrested that criminal sergeant-major of the *Kempeitai*[1] as soon as you arrived, everyone was delighted. They want to return to normal times and finish with the Japanese and with terrorists. But I tell you this: if the people are going to help you, they must see you rule.' He struck the arm of the chair with his fist. 'If they see you are weak they will be afraid. One more thing. Let us hope that you have come to stay. In 1942 the Allies fled and left us to the Japanese; now we are afraid you will go away again and leave us to the Javanese.'

How often during the following months was I to hear those same opinions voiced by Balinese of every caste and rank! In my naive ignorance it never occurred to me that they had any ground for such fears, let alone that they were speaking with the voice of prophecy.

The guards I posted must have looked formidable enough to deter Sukawati's enemies, for there were no more attempts on his safety. He remained in seclusion until the arrival of the Dutch, when he put his exceptional qualities at their disposal, rendering great service to them and to

---

[1] Japanese Security Policy. The arrest was ordered by the 5th Indian Division.

his own people. When the Dutch handed over power in 1947 to the Indonesian Federation he was elected President of the State of East Indonesia, which included Celebes, Bali and Lombok, with the capital at Macassar. But after the suppression of this State by the Javanese Central Government of Dr. Sukarno—in flagrant breach of the treaty with the Dutch—Sukawati retired from political life; when I last heard of him he was doing very well as a motor-car salesman in Djakarta.

As soon as I had given orders for the posting of the guards I signalled General Mansergh, asking for authority to arrest the terrorist leaders and hold them until the arrival of the Dutch; also to publish a proclamation I had drafted inviting the co-operation of all Balinese in the maintenance of order. Permission came back immediately for the arrests, with the express proviso that they must be carried out by Japanese troops. I was categorically forbidden to issue any proclamation.

The arrests, however, proved far from easy to achieve. Whether they foresaw my intentions or whether, as is very probable, they had allies among the Japanese, many of the wanted men disappeared; some fled to remote villages, others went into hiding in the neighbourhood. In the meantime, from Den Pasar and from Tabanan to the west came more reports of the murder or disappearance of Balinese officials and headmen supposed to be unsympathetic to the extremists. Our own servants became frightened to work for us, and one or two left our service, although the crowd of sightseers outside our gates never seemed to diminish. In time we laid hands on some of the men we wanted, and the example of a few arrests brought a rapid improvement in the situation.

I had given orders to the Japanese that these prisoners should be well treated; that they might see their families, who could bring them extra food; but that they might receive no other visitors or have any other contact with the outside world. One evening I walked round to the prison with Miura to see how my orders were being carried out. Each of the prisoners had a cell to himself. When I interviewed them in the courtyard they greeted me with smiling politeness and assured me that they had no complaints to make of their treatment. However, when I remarked that I was sorry to meet them in such circumstances their reply was scarcely reassuring.

'We do not at all mind being here,' laughed their spokesman. 'We know that we must suffer to win our freedom. After all, the great leaders of the Russian revolution were often in prison before they came to power.'

'Do you then mean to follow the examples of Lenin and Stalin,' I asked, 'when you win this freedom you talk about?'

They smiled again, but gave me no answer.

I pondered sadly on the strange contradiction whereby men who will gladly become martyrs in the cause of freedom will invoke the name of freedom, when they themselves achieve power, to persecute their own people. The result in Indonesia was to impose a heavier oppression than any endured under the Dutch.

With a heavy heart I strolled back in the twilight to the more cheerful atmosphere of the Residency, where Shaw with the help of fresh limes was converting some of our operational rum into a badly needed drink.

In the afternoon, a few hours after my visit to Tjokorde Sukawati, I was sitting in my office, drafting a long signal and pausing occasionally to look longingly out of the window at the sunlight glistening on the palm fronds still dripping from a rain-storm, and to sniff the damp, heavy-scented air that drifted in from the garden; Shaw was discussing with Colonel Tsuneoka the location of supply dumps; Neville was at the beach-head. From the hall outside came the burr and tapping of the wireless.

This quiet scene of industry and application was suddenly interrupted by a series of sharp, urgent commands in Japanese from the drive; a moment later there was a quick knock and a young lieutenant stood saluting in the doorway. He spoke rapidly to Colonel Tsuneoka. Miura turned to me.

'Sir, we have heard that rebellion has broken out at Gianjar: the Rajah has just telephoned to one of our posts. He says that a force of three hundred extremist elements has assembled south of Gianjar and is marching against him; they have some rifles and spears. The Rajah is very alarmed and asks your help.'

I turned to Shaw. 'This, I imagine, is the kind of situation General Mansergh had in mind when he warned me against the indiscriminate use of force. Somehow we must settle this affair without bloodshed, and I see only one way to do it—to go there ourselves and try to parley with the rebels. I only hope they won't be in the mood to shoot first and parley afterwards! Now will you collect a couple of Buffs and tell Shimada to get the Chevrolet ready? I'll get Tsuneoka to send round a lorry-load of Nips with a light machine-gun to keep us company.'

By four o'clock we were ready to start. Shaw and I sat in the front of the staff car with Shimada; the two Buffs, as happy as schoolboys on a treat, sat with Miura in the back, one armed with a Sten, the other nursing a rifle. Ten solemn-faced Japanese infantrymen under a subaltern followed in their lorry.

Infected with the cheerfulness of our two soldiers I felt a thrill of excitement at the thought that now I was really on my mettle, and that on the decisions I might have to make in the next few hours would probably rest the peace and security of the island. On the other hand I could not suppress a twinge of dismay when I contemplated the possible cost in lives if a mistake or misjudgment on my part should let this revolt get out of hand; I cannot deny that I was also daunted by the ignoble thought of how my own reputation would suffer in the eyes of General Mansergh and the world if I should fail—although I was unlikely to survive to endure the disgrace. What, after all, did I yet know of these people? In particular, what did I know, beyond a vague report by telephone, of the situation I was driving so lightheartedly to meet?

It was this last thought that steadied me, with the reflection that there was nothing more I could do or plan to do until I arrived on the spot and saw the situation for myself. I should have to play it off the cuff; meanwhile, I had better relax and enjoy the scenery.

We passed through Kesiman with its low mud walls and thatched gateways, where men squatted in groups by the roadside idling and gossiping; the women were returning from the market carrying loads in baskets on their heads, the girls proud and erect as goddesses, graceful as nymphs, each with an arm raised to balance the weight of the basket. Beyond the village, as we drove east, the palm trees gave way to ricefields, where the vivid green of the young paddy blended with the rich gold of the ripening crop. War and rebellion seemed far away.

'I find it encouraging,' Shaw broke in upon my thoughts, 'to see people on the roads and in the fields. In Java you always knew there was trouble afoot if the countryside was deserted and the men were not working in the *sawas*'

'Yes, but we've still a fair way to go. What I'm wondering is whether we're going to find that this is the start of a full-scale revolt by the *Pemudas*, which is what the Rajah would have us believe, or whether it's just a local riot by some of the lads who don t like the Rajah or don't want to pay his taxes; Gianjar, you remember, was one of the few Rajahs whom the Dutch allowed to retain most of their feudal rights after the conquest of South Bali. Anyway, I don't suppose we'll be left long in doubt.'

We climbed gently among the terraced fields, on a well-constructed metalled road shaded by great sugar palms. Approaching Gianjar we saw immediately that something was wrong. Groups of young men carrying long spears and heavy *koloks*, or chopping knives, thronged the road, padding silently in the direction of the Rajah's Palace; they were naked except for their loincloths girt up above their knees, and they looked resolute and grim. They paid no attention to us whatever.

Puzzled as to whether we were among enemies or friends, I told Shimada to drive on slowly to the palace; the throng of Balinese made way for us reluctantly but without sparing us more than a glance. I felt the tension rising as we drove through them, and wondered whether at any moment we were to meet the fate of poor Brigadier Mallaby. Quite suddenly, as the last group parted before us, I saw ahead the square of Gianjar and the carved gateway of the Rajah's *puri*, or palace. Under the broad, cascading *waringin*[1] in front of

---

[1] The giant banyan tree, sacred to the Hindus; its great branches droop to the ground, where they form new roots to spread the girth of the tree. In every Balinese

it stood a slight figure in a grey uniform with a Sam Browne belt and a pistol holster; the pistol, a Luger, was in his hand. We halted as he hastened towards us.

His Highness Anak Agung Gdé Agung, 'Child of the Great Grand Great', acting Rajah of Gianjar and eldest son of the old ruler, was a slim, handsome man of about thirty, with a sensitive face, bright, intelligent eyes, dark, curly hair and small, sad moustache; his nervous manner seemed inappropriate to his smartly cut military tunic and breeches. As I stepped from my car to salute him he replaced his Luger in its holster—to my great relief—and shook me warmly by the hand.

'I think you have come only just in time.' His English was careful but fluent, his voice soft and hesitant. 'The concentrations of Pemudas have increased since this morning, and now there are at least two thousand of them. My own people are loyal to me—you passed many of them just now on the road, coming here to defend me—but there are not enough of us; besides, the enemy have rifles, while I am the only one here to possess a gun. I have been trying to warn you since midday, but it took me so long to get a message through.'

'How did this trouble start?' I asked.

'It has been in preparation for a long time, but I think your arrival in Bali hastened the event. It is organized by the *Sukerela*, the extremist leaders in Den Pasar. You see, Gianjar is the richest, and most populated part of Bali, and if they can gain control here they think they will be too powerful for you to overthrow them. So they have assembled men from Badung and Tabanan to attack me and my people. But we will resist them to the end!'

'Where are they assembled?'

'If you follow that road southward through the *sawas* you will come upon my outposts; I will send a man with you that far, to see they let you pass. When you have passed them you will see the Pemudas within a few hundred metres—but please be careful, because I fear they will shoot at you before they know who you are.'

Leaving the *Anak Agung* to complete the organization of his defences we turned down the road he had indicated; his guide perched on the mudguard. As we passed more groups of spearmen I recalled the stories I had read of the palace retainers who had thrown themselves with their gold-tipped spears upon the Dutch riflemen when the Rajahs of South Bali went down in mass suicide before the European invaders.

We came into a countryside of open paddy-fields on either side of the road. On a corner a small group of spearmen barred our way, waving to us

---

village square there are *waringin*, beneath which are performed the plays and dances at festivals.

with urgent gestures. Miura and our guide exchanged a few words with them, then Miura said to me:

'This is the last of the Rajah's outposts. They say that we shall find the *Pemudas* a short way down the road. They ask us not to go on, because we shall be attacked.'

I ordered the Japanese to get out of their lorry and precede us along the road in open file; at the same time I told their subaltern that there was to be no shooting unless we were fired upon. When they were fifty yards ahead I told Shimada to drive on slowly. Leaving the Rajah's guide with the picket looking gloomily after us, we continued our journey; I was feeling far from happy, but it was clearly essential for us to make contact with the Pemudas, and quickly.

We made it quicker than I had expected. At one moment there was nobody in sight; at the next we were confronted with a road block of felled trees and, behind it, a mob of sullen-looking Balinese; most were armed and clad like the Rajah's retainers, but a few among them were dressed in green shirts and slacks and I noticed with misgiving that these men, whom I assumed to be the leaders, carried rifles or pistols. Many more Pemudas were dispersed among the paddy on either side of the road.

The Japanese halted and took up action stations; the subaltern hurried back to me for orders, his concern showing plainly on his face. As Shimada stopped the car I scrambled out, followed immediately by Shaw, the two Buffs and, more slowly, Miura.

'This is where we parley—I hope.' I smiled to Shaw and started to walk towards the road block. The lieutenant stood in front of me, saluting and talking urgently in Japanese.

'He begs you not to go forward, sir,' translated Miura. 'He says he is responsible for your safety.'

'Tell him he's also under my orders. He's to stay here with his men until I tell him to move.'

Leaving the Buffs by the car Shaw and I approached the *Pemudas*; we put on the most nonchalant air we could muster, but for my part I know that my stomach felt full of butterflies and, as the Spaniards so prettily express it, my testicles were in my throat. Once again I thought of Brigadier Mallaby and the appalling massacre that had followed his murder; as always in moments of acute peril, I found myself praying to the God I usually neglected.

There was a stir in the ranks behind the barricade and my tortured stomach contracted again as I saw the spearmen stiffen at their leaders' commands; there was a murmur of voices, in which I caught the words '*Orang Puteh*'[1] Then quite suddenly and without warning relaxation spread like a ripple along the lowering faces in front of us; there were cries of '*tabeh, tuan!*'

---

[1] 'White men'—in Malay, not Balinese

and several men gave us the Merdeka salute. Two youths in European dress climbed nimbly over the road block and ran up to us with hands outstretched in greeting; others followed until we were the centre of a crowd, who studied us with silent but apparently not hostile interest.

I had been turning over in my mind what I should say, and had improvised a simple speech on the lines of the proclamation I had wished to publish. The details would make dull reading at this distance, but in essence it was a plea for the co-operation of all Balinese in the maintenance of peace, an assurance that we would do all in our power to restore prosperity to the island and a veiled threat that I would not hesitate to use force if I found it necessary; I concluded with the platitude that on their co-operation depended the quick removal of the Japanese forces, and urged them to disperse to their homes without delay.

When I had finished there was silence for a few moments. Then came the expected question.

'Will the Dutch come back, or shall we be allowed to govern ourselves?'

I knew the answer to that one. 'The Allied governments will decide in consultation the future of Bali in the best interests of the Balinese people.' I made Miura repeat the last three words, while I looked pointedly at the half-dozen Javanese we had noticed among the leaders.

There was a brief discussion among the *Pemudas*; soon they began to drift away southward in small groups, giving us their salute as they went. I was not so sanguine as to suppose that they were going home.

'I think I'll stay in Gianjar,' I told Shaw, 'in case they attack during the night. Miura and the Nips will have to stay too, and I'll have another platoon sent here at once from Klungkung. Will you take our party back to Den Pasar and send a signal to Surabaja giving all details? Shimada can come back to collect me in the morning.'

'You ought to go back and send the signal,' protested Shaw, 'and let me stay here. If it comes to a battle I know much more about soldiering than you do.'

'Maybe. But if it comes to a battle I dare say the Nip commander is a reasonably competent infantry officer. I want to be here to watch how the situation develops.'

We found the *Anak Agung* pacing anxiously before the palace; his men were ranged in lines around the square, squatting on the ground with their long spears held upright before them. He was grateful but far from reassured.

'I am certain they have not gone away,' he declared gloomily.

'They are sure to attack during the night.'

He cheered up when I suggested that I should stay, and disappeared into the palace to see personally to my comfort. I said good-bye to Shaw and two almost mutinous Buffs, who clearly felt themselves cheated of their fun; Shaw's parting handshake was a little too firm and 'stiff upper lip' for my comfort, and I watched the Chevrolet disappear in the twilight with a curious feeling of desolation. It was going to be an anxious night. The telephone between Gianjar and Klungkung had broken down—more probably it had been cut—and so my demand for reinforcements would have to be sent by radio from Japanese headquarters in Den Pasar. It was unlikely that help would arrive before morning; meanwhile we had only the small force I had brought with me, and about two hundred of the Rajah's retainers, to oppose at least ten times as many *Pemudas*, some of whom were armed with modern rifles. Having stationed the Japanese in the square outside the palace, where they would be under my immediate control in case of attack, I went inside to have supper with the *Anak Agung*.

Although it was an excellent meal neither of us felt like eating; but courtesy obliged us both to try. The *Anak Agung* was the most intelligent and best educated of the Rajahs—in fact about the most intelligent Balinese I met.[1] We talked, inevitably, of nationalism and the future of Indonesia, on which I was particularly anxious to learn his views. He praised the efficiency of pre-war Dutch administration and the selfless devotion of their best Residents and Controllers; but he was critical of some aspects of their educational policy, in particular their suppression of all political activity, which had provided the Japanese with a useful field for exploitation.

'We hope for independence, of course,' he explained. 'But not the kind of *merdeka* preached by those hot-headed boys in Den Pasar!'

He spoke of the Council of Rajahs, through which the Dutch had to some degree governed Bali; and it occurred to me then that the Council might prove the answer to my own problem of establishing a temporary civilian administration. I decided to explore the possibility as soon as the present trouble was over.

When we had finished eating we went to bed; the Rajah led me to the guest pavilion, a miniature bungalow on the opposite side of the courtyard from the main building of the palace; its single room was plainly but comfortably furnished.

'I hope I shall wake up if there is an attack.' I tried to put on an air of indifference. 'I should be ashamed to sleep through a battle!'

'Do not worry. If there is an alarm we beat the *kulkul*—the great drum in the tower above. Nobody can sleep through that noise.'

I took off my belt and pistol and boots, and stretched out on the divan bed. For all my pretence to the *Anak Agung* I felt no inclination to sleep. My thoughts were chaotic, my mind torn between anxiety over the hazards of

---

[1] Subsequently he became Indonesian Foreign Minister under Sukarno; he has also held appointments of Indonesian Ambassador in Paris and in Brussels. Later he quarrelled with Sukarno, but he still has a desk in the Ministry of Foreign Affairs in Djakarta.

the coming night and a childlike, even snobbish elation at the glamorous circumstances in which I found myself—a guest in the palace of a powerful feudal prince, surrounded by enemies from whom I was pledged to protect him. I began to wonder whether the Anak Aging's hospitality would extend to providing me with a beautiful Balinese girl to share my bed; I had heard such stories before,[1] and confess that I kept my ears pricked for some sound that might herald the arrival of a concubine. . . .

It was a different sound that woke me a few hours later: the deep, urgent throbbing of the *kulkul*, its fast, panicky beats bursting through the heavy pall of my unconsciousness. A blaze of light appeared in the doorway, where I saw a servant in a girded loin-cloth carrying a flaming resin torch and beckoning me urgently to get up; I struggled into my boots and ran out after him, buckling my belt on the way.

Outside, the great *waringin* threw its dark, domed shadow across the moon-drenched square; its smooth leaves reflected the soft silvery light in a thousand tiny stars. The Anak Agung was giving orders to a group of his chiefs and *pungawas*; most of his retainers had vanished—I hoped to battle stations—but a small bodyguard remained by the tree. I walked over to the Japanese, who sprang to attention at my approach. The subaltern looked at me attentively, awaiting orders; Miura stood beside him, looking at the ground. Having satisfied myself that they were ready to go into action at once, I joined the *Anak Agung*. Despite his obvious anxiety he preserved an admirable self-control and when he spoke his tone was calm and resolute.

'The attack is coming in from the south, from the direction of the road block you saw this evening; they have been concentrating there for the last half-hour—I could see the lights of their torches from the tower. We must be ready to fight. I have sent my men to their posts.'

I called Miura and the Japanese subaltern, explained the situation to them and told the subaltern to take up a position commanding the enemy line of advance. As soon as the *Pemudas* came within easy range the machine-gunner was to fire three separate bursts over their heads; if they still continued to advance the whole section would open fire to kill.

'We may be few,' I tried to reassure the *Anak Agung* as the soldiers trotted off into the darkness, 'but I doubt if the *Pemudas* will stand up very long to machine-gun fire.'

'Let us hope,' he answered glumly.

We stood together in silence, listening for some sound that would tell us the attack had started. But no human voice or noise of battle broke the tense, uneasy stillness of that lovely night; only the shrill humming of the cicadas

---

[1] There was truth in them, too. Dr. Jacobs records that during his visit to Gianjar in 1882 the women of the harem were instructed to make themselves agreeable to him and his party every night. Some people have all the luck.

strummed a ceaseless accompaniment to our gloomy thoughts. Moonlight flooded the countryside that sloped away to the south-west in numerous narrow ravines, and glittered silver on the smooth sheets of water covering the terraced ricefields; the air was soft and heavy with the sweet, intoxicating fragrance of champaka flowers—the strong, heady smell of the Balinese night.

From close at hand came a burst of machine-gun fire, followed five seconds later by another, and then a third; in the ensuing silence we looked at one another long and hard.

'We are about to see,' I smiled grimly as I moved towards the Japanese, 'whether what I told you just now was right.'

Suddenly I halted in my tracks. From the east, faintly at first but rapidly growing louder, I heard the sound of engines: motor transport approaching at speed from the direction of Klungkung; in a few moments the lights of a convoy came into view. At the same time a runner padded up from the Japanese lieutenant with the news that the enemy had halted after the three bursts from his machine-gun; on the approach of the convoy they had begun to withdraw. A long line of lorries drove into the square and ground to a halt; instead of the platoon I had demanded, there was a full company of infantry, well equipped with light machine-guns and mortars. Clearly somebody had been using his initiative. The danger was over; half an hour later I was back in bed.

Before leaving in the morning I gave orders that a company of Japanese should be stationed permanently in Gianjar; it was as well that I did, because next day there were two separate attacks on the town. The Japanese garrison repulsed them, but did not prevent the *Pemudas* from pillaging and burning houses in several villages around; the Japanese commander, misinterpreting my instructions, had been reluctant to open fire and had preferred to withdraw his troops into the town. Thereafter I amended my orders to allow him to open fire on all *Pemuda* concentrations that did not disperse after one warning volley.

IX

PAINTERS AND PRINCES

My first action on returning to Den Pasar was to signal General Mansergh asking permission to entrust the civil administration of the island to the Council of Rajahs; my second was to summon the Council to meet at Klungkung the following afternoon. Late the same night I received a reply from the General giving his full approval to my plan; another signal warned us that the Dutch would land at 8 a.m. on 2nd March.

Apart from the visit to Gianjar our duties had hitherto confined us to the Den Pasar area; it was time, I judged, for us to see what was going on in other parts of the island. We had less than three days before the landing, and so could only hope to cover the more important districts. I therefore decided to visit Singaradja that same afternoon, the 27th, for as yet I knew nothing of the situation in North Bali; on my way back I would call in at the village of Kintamani, on the rim of the volcano Batur, and see the Austrian painter Roland Strasser, who had lived there throughout the Japanese occupation. Meanwhile I asked Shaw to take the other staff car to Klungkung and Karangasem in the east; he could combine the journey with a visit to the Swiss artist Theo Meier, who lived at Iseh in the foothills of Gunung Agung.

As soon as I had dealt with the signal traffic I set out, taking a few sandwiches to eat in the car in order to save time. We drove through Gianjar, then turned north towards the mountains along a straight, palm-fringed avenue that rose in a gentle gradient among terraces of paddy. Above the neat and peaceful village of Bangli, at a height of nearly two thousand feet, the lush vegetation and rich *sawas* gave way to rough hill pasture; poinsettias grew thickly by the roadside, winding up the hill in a ribbon of scarlet. Soon we began to climb steeply. The air grew suddenly colder and the sky overcast; to the east a dark mass of lowering cloud hid the gigantic cone of Gunung Agung.

A fierce and bitter wind howled across the mountainside, hurling great gusts of rain against our windscreen; with every mile the stony landscape became bleaker, the few villages more miserable and dirty. Shivering in my thin clothes I could scarcely believe that we had only just left the tropical exuberance of South Bali. Above three thousand feet the pass was in cloud, which limited our vision to fifty yards and hid the great bulk of Batur and its crater lake. Round a corner we came upon two wild-looking men riding scraggy ponies—the first travellers we had met in this desolate region; they pulled hurriedly off the road and, huddled and hooded in their thick blankets, watched us go by, neither acknowledging our greeting nor showing any sign of interest in our appearance.

'Not very friendly, are they?' called out Sergeant Hopkins from the back; he had asked to come with me for the ride. 'Do you think they know who we are?'

'No, and I don't suppose they care either. It must be all the same to these highlanders whether the Dutch, the Nips, the British or their own people are in power. Nobody seems to have bothered about them; they look as if they live pretty near the starvation level, and I'm sure they wouldn't recognize a social conscience if they saw one.'

The head of the pass marked the boundary with North Bali—the Residency of Singaradja and the ancient State of Buleleng.[1] From this point the road wound steeply down towards the north coast; the mist dispersed and the grim mountain landscape gave place to terraced paddy-fields, their crops a lustreless green under the overcast sky. We entered Singaradja along a broad, straight avenue flanked by the neat but neglected European bungalows of the old Colonial administration, and turned in, through stone gateposts adorned by two enormous carved snakes, to the drive-way of the Residency.

Here the Rajah, warned by telephone of my visit, was awaiting me with his brother. Both of them spoke English and both, I believe, were graduates of the University of Leyden. The Rajah, who seemed a man of initiative and intelligence, told me that he had already taken command of the native police and, with the co-operation of the Japanese, was keeping order in his territory; there were no incidents to report. He welcomed me warmly and promised me all the help in his power; but, like Sukawati a few days before, he was frankly apprehensive about the future course of Allied policy.

'I am afraid you are going to hand us over to the Javanese,' he predicted. And his brother added with a wry smile, 'Bali has been called "the last Paradise". Will it become "the lost Paradise"?'

The clouds were still down over Batur when we reached Kintamani. The house of Roland Strasser, built in the style of an Alpine chalet, stood a little way apart from the village, alone and cheerless in that rain-soaked mountain scene. Despite their friendly greeting, I was shocked by the forlorn appearance of the artist and his Hungarian wife; in contrast to the carefree, ebullient Le Mayeurs they seemed worn out by illness, adversity and fear. Their nationality and status as 'friendly aliens' had given them little protection from the venom of the Japanese, who had subjected them to ceaseless petty

---

[1] Although Singaradja was the Dutch administrative capital of the island, the adjacent port of Buleleng was the seat of the Balinese Rajah.

persecution, and none from the rapacity of the local villagers, who had taken advantage of their distress and loneliness to pillage and insult them.

'I *hate* these people!' Strasser's rugged features twisted with indignation and disgust. 'They are *despicable*—vicious, treacherous and cruel!' His tall, bowed frame shook and the tufts of grey hair at the side of his bald head stood out like the wings on a Norseman's helmet.

'Now all we want is to go away from here,' murmured his wife, a gentle, slim blonde whose pretty face was marred with the pallor of sickness. 'We should like to go to America, or even back to Europe—anywhere outside Asia, and especially away from Bali with its hateful memories.'

Privately I thought that I too might come to hate Bali if I had chosen to seclude myself among these dark and storm-swept hills. But Strasser took me aside and whispered urgently, 'Erica is very ill indeed. She must have an operation—a very serious operation you understand—as quickly as possible. I implore you, colonel, to do something to get us away from here.'

Overcome with pity by the urgency and despair in his voice I gladly undertook to do what I could for them. As soon as the Dutch arrived and we had the Kuta airstrip in use, I thought it should be possible to fly them to Java; meanwhile I offered to send a truck in the morning to bring them to the comparative comfort and safety of Den Pasar, where at least we had better medical facilities than they enjoyed at Kintamani. But they would not hear of leaving their house and possessions to be looted, and preferred to remain for the moment at Kintamani. Later on, however, they made their way to Den Pasar, where I was able to introduce them to General Mansergh during his visit; he immediately had them flown in his personal aircraft to Surabaja and thence to Australia. The operation on Frau Strasser was successful, and they now live happily in California.

The mood of despondency brought upon me by my visit to this stricken pair evaporated as we came down from the mountains and the mist, and saw below us in the evening light the richly coloured pattern of ricefields and palm groves falling away towards the sea in tier after tier of green and gold. By the roadside between Bangli and Gianjar men and women were bathing in the ditches and streams, splashing, laughing and chattering happily. Less pleasing were the numbers of miserable dogs, with mangy coats and ulcerous backs, that thronged the approaches to each village—the outcast, scavenging offspring of the watchdogs kept by every Balinese household; at night their howling chorus keeps away the witches.

Near Gianjar we saw a file of ducks strutting across the fields, making their way homeward in neat and orderly column behind an old man who carried an improvised flag—a bamboo topped with a bunch of white feathers. Balinese ducks are curiously well trained: every morning, soon after sunrise, they march out from the village to feed in the ricefields, following in perfect formation behind their herdsman, an old man or a child carrying a white flag; when they reach their feeding place the herdsman plants the flag in the ground and returns to his other duties. The ducks will stay near the flag all day, eating the weeds and insects that damage the rice but never touching the shoots. In the evening, half an hour before sundown, the herdsman returns and picks up the flag; the ducks assemble round him and strut off in solemn procession behind him to the village.

Here in Bali, as in the Greece of Sappho, evening was gathering in all that bright morning scattered. Huge water buffaloes, dark grey or pale pink, lumbered and slouched their way home, each of them led or ridden by a tiny, naked urchin in a preposterously large straw sun-hat shaped like an inverted shallow bowl. These powerful and treacherous brutes never seem to turn their ill-temper against the little boys who look after them; but to adults, and to Europeans in particular, they are notoriously dangerous—which may account for the saying, once popular in India, that 'the ugliest creatures in the East are water buffaloes and British officers' wives'.

Shaw reported extremely satisfactory interviews with the Rajahs of Klungkung and Karangasem; both had promised us their full support, the Dewa Agung adding that he was 'looking forward eagerly to the day when the Dutch should return and restore normal conditions', a remark on which Shaw had wisely declined to comment. From the Swiss painter at Iseh he brought me enthusiastic messages of welcome and a pressing invitation to pay him a visit.

'I should certainly go when you get a chance,' he added. 'Theo Meier's an extraordinary little man—full of energy and vivacity. Knows a lot about Bali too, and is extremely popular with the villagers. He runs a sort of amateur clinic at Iseh, and has his own Home Guard to protect him from the *Pemudas*; he also has his own home-made arak, which he calls "Swhisky"—and I reckon you need something to protect you from that! In fact he seems to do pretty well, one way and another; he has the most glamorous collection of girls in his house, not the least glamorous of them being his wife.'

'She's Balinese, isn't she?'

'Yes, she comes from Sanoer. I don't quite know who the rest of them are—in-laws, servants or concubines, I suppose. But seriously, Peter, you ought to go and take a look for yourself. They're well worth the journey on their own account.'

'How's the political situation up there?'

'Quiet, for the moment. Theo's given me a long document to pass on to you, explaining his views on the state of Bali and how we ought to run the place. I don't know if you'll be able to make head or tail of it; it runs on, rather like his conversation, in a mixture of English, French, German, and Malay, with a few Balinese phrases thrown in for luck.'

'Well, I'll certainly drop in on him as soon as I see an opportunity. Quite apart from the Swhisky and the harem—and don't think I'm not keen to have a taste of the one and at least a glance at the other—he sounds as though he would well repay a visit. But I don't see how we can fit it in before the landing the day after tomorrow.'

I sat down to digest the twelve closely written pages of fool-scap which Theo Meier had sent me—not an easy task in view of the strange mixture of languages in which they were written and the very curious syntax and spelling of the English. However, I read them carefully, because I knew from Daan Hubrecht that Meier had lived eight years in the island; that he had acquired an intimate knowledge of the folklore and customs of the people; and that he enjoyed the friendship and confidence of all castes and classes, being one of the few Europeans who had taken the trouble to learn their language—or rather languages. In general his thesis served to confirm what I had already heard from other sources—that we must lose no time in asserting our authority and showing the people that we meant to rule. I will quote a few extracts.

> 'I have nothing to do with ruling Bali,' he wrote, 'but I learn from the facts that are happening in Den Pasar today. Please learn it too and take the tragic consequence—*and be strong now*. . . . Being strong now means no bloodshed, but in a week it may be impossible without. . . . Oriental people have no respect for weakness in cases like these [the murders around Den Pasar], and your land "humane" behaviour is just *mistaken as weak*, and no oriental people trusts or believes in or even honours weakness. All my Balinese friends are afraid about your weakness. . . . Act now, rule as strong as possible and then make *for ever* friends in keeping your word of giving them freedom, when there is peace.'

I was disconcerted to learn that I had given such a widespread impression of weakness; there was little I could do about it in the two days still left to me before the arrival of the Dutch. But at least, it seemed, we were not unpopular.

> 'Freedom not believed [sic],' he went on. 'But 99% of Bali wants you, believe in you. A high Pedanda[1] told me today: "If you like Bali, come and rule in its greatest moment of *susah* [trouble], and when is *aman* [peace] give us the present of our country. But conquer first." My friend the Pungawa of Selat said nearly the same. . . . Don't ask any more if the Balinese officials want to work with you and the

---

[1] Brahmana high priest.

Rajahs now. Take it for normal that they do and make it plenty hard known to them that they stand trial for murder—or helping murder—if not working. Every day lost means that most of the loyal Balinese functionaries lose confidence in your, the Rajahs', and their own power and influence. After a few years of Japanese terror most functionaries' nerves are near a breakdown, and only medicine is immediate personal contact with you and strongest actions against crime.'

This absorbing document impressed me by its humility no less than its sincerity: 'As I am no man with any knowledge of economic and without any education for administration, I cannot give you "logique" advises, but just the result of my artist-mind.' There was a touching postscript: '*Now take no risk more!* Take Theo Meier the ink and paper away; give him brush and colour and buy his paintings.'

In the morning, accompanied by the Japanese commanders, we went to inspect the beach-head, which Neville had pronounced ready for the assault landing. I was astonished at the transformation his ingenuity had wrought, in so short a time, on that rock- and boulder-strewn beach and scrub-covered foreshore; now, with every natural obstacle cleared or blasted away, it might have formed part of some fashionable Lido. Connecting the beach-head with the road from Den Pasar Neville had built a wide dirt track suitable for motor traffic. When I had given my final orders for the deployment of the Japanese troops guarding the approaches we returned to Den Pasar to prepare for the Rajahs' conference that afternoon.

It was in a state of considerable anxiety that I set out for Klungkung, after an early and hasty lunch which I had no appetite to eat. So much depended on the outcome of this conference. In my optimistic plan for presenting the Dutch, on their arrival, with an efficient and smoothly-working civil administration I had taken it for granted that all the Rajahs would support me. But would they? It was just as likely that some of them would be hostile, and even more likely that some would hedge; they might be sympathetic to this new spirit of xenophobic nationalism, or unwilling to risk the wrath of the terrorists, who had already shown that they were not afraid to strike at the great. Of one thing only could I be sure—that in the game of statecraft and political manoeuvre these princes would have forgotten more than I should ever learn.

Xenophobic nationalism, of course, might equally operate in my favour; my impression was that the majority of them, like most of their subjects, feared Javanese more than European rule, and there was no doubt that the terrorists took their orders from Java. The Japanese, on the other hand, were universally un-popular, and I could expect opposition to the use of Japanese troops in support of our government. I hated the idea myself, but what alternative did we have? The native police were unarmed and it would take time to arm them in sufficient numbers; nor did I know how many of them were reliable. For the moment, however distasteful the thought, the Japanese were my only means of keeping order. I was still reviewing the situation when we drew up outside the palace at Klungkung.

Only two out of the eight members of the Council were absent: the Rajah of the western state of Djembrana had sent a message pleading illness, and the aged and infirm Rajah of Badung (Den Pasar) was represented by his eldest son. When the introductions were over we took our seats at a long table; the *Dewa Agung* of Klungkung, a dignified and portly figure in white robes, sat at the head, with me and my interpreter on his right. Behind each rajah stood a court official, presumably of Brahmana caste, in the role of secretary. Some of the older men wore richly embroidered Balinese dress, in contrast to the carefully pressed white shirts and trousers of the emancipated young.

Striving to control my nervousness I rose to address them. Speaking slowly, with long pauses at the end of each sentence to allow the interpreter to translate and my audience to assimilate what I was saying, I began with a brief explanation of the purpose of my mission; I outlined the main problems, as I saw them, and my reasons for inviting the rajahs to take over the civil administration in their respective areas; and in conclusion, with all the force and eloquence I could command, I launched my plea for their support.

A long debate followed, in which the principal point of argument, as I had foreseen, was the weakness of the native police and the necessity for making use of the Japanese. In the end it was the *Dewa Agung* who swayed the meeting to my side.

'Will you promise us,' he asked me, 'that you will give us arms for our police?'

'Tuanku *Dewa Agung*,' I answered, 'I will signal my headquarters tonight, asking permission from my general.'

'Very well then,' he continued. 'As the English colonel said earlier, it will take time to have our own police armed and ready. In the meantime order must be preserved. It is regrettable that we should have to use the Japanese; but surely, my friends, it is better to use them for a little while than to watch Bali disintegrate before our eyes in bloodshed, anarchy and civil war!'

One by one the others rose to speak their approval. There was only one voice raised in opposition: the young son of the Rajah of Badung sprang to his feet and delivered a violent attack on me, my policy and my methods.

'It is shameful to use Japanese soldiers to suppress the *Pemudas*, who only ask for freedom!' he shouted. 'The *Pemudas* would not be active if the Japanese did not hunt them all the time. I want no Japanese guards in Den

Pasar!' He glared at me out of bright and angry eyes. 'Take away your soldiers, bring the *Pemudas* into the administration, and you will have no trouble!'

He spoke with such passion and sincerity that, despite my indignation, I could scarcely refrain from clapping when he sat down. However, much as I admired his courage I could not ignore the implications of his speech, especially when I learned that he was a leader of one of the extreme revolutionary groups in Den Pasar. Fortunately his outburst seemed to have little effect on the other Rajahs, who agreed to give the necessary orders to their *pungawas* immediately.

After the conference was over the *Dewa Agung* took me to see the famous Kerta Gosa, the court-house of Klungkung. This ancient building, a simple but beautifully carved and decorated pavilion, stood at a crossroads in the centre of the town. A stair-case guarded by two stone serpents led to a raised platform covered by a roof and fenced by a stone balustrade along each side, the ceiling was covered with paintings illustrating the tortures of the damned in hell—evidently the work of an artist, or artists, of a sadistic turn of mind.

The *kertas* are the courts of the Rajahs, and the judges are usually Brahmana priests; but the people only appeal to them as a last resort, in cases of particular complexity or bitterness, preferring to settle their disputes within the village community. I never witnessed any proceedings before a *kerta*, but I am told that their rules and technical language resemble those of the cockfight which is such an important feature of Balinese life. There is, however, nothing lighthearted about the ritual of swearing-in. The oath is administered to only one of the contesting parties—the judges determine which one—in an elaborate and extremely solemn ceremony, and invokes appalling calamities upon the person and family of a perjurer. The judges also pay particular attention to the bearing and mannerisms of the litigants during the trial, noting any signs of nervousness, hesitation or anxiety.

I returned to Den Pasar in a mood of considerable satisfaction, bordering upon elation, very different from the gloom in which I had left earlier that afternoon. With the exception of Badung and possibly Djembrana, who had been absent, I felt I could now depend upon the Rajahs' support; the Dutch should find at least a foundation on which to build. My first action on reaching my headquarters was to put the eldest son of the Rajah of Badung under house arrest in his father's palace, and to instruct the Japanese to keep him under surveillance. I regretted having to take this step against a sincere and courageous young man, but he was already suspected of helping the terrorists in the town and of organizing the movement of *Pemudas* towards Gianjar which had caused trouble earlier; he was obviously in a position to cause further trouble, and I could afford to take no risks at such a time. In the circumstances I could hardly be accused of undue severity. I also told the Japanese to increase their day and night patrols in an effort to stop the movement of *Pemudas* to Gianjar, and to increase their watch on the Javanese in the town, from whom I was sure we had most to fear.

There was a signal in from Surabaja informing me that we were to remain in Bali for a week after the arrival of the Dutch, during which period I was to act as political adviser to Colonel Ter Meulen; General Mansergh would arrive in *Loch Eck* on the 8th to accept the official surrender of the Japanese forces at a ceremonial parade on the Alun-Alun.

Both Shaw and I had been impressed by the excellent discipline of the Japanese in Bali; on this particular evening I caught a glimpse of the methods by which it was maintained. Walking past a building occupied by Japanese troops near the Residency I was amazed to see the sentry, instead of springing to attention at my approach, remain standing at ease, watching me with an unmistakably impudent leer. I had been warned in Surabaja to be particularly strict in enforcing the orders requiring all Japanese ranks to salute Allied officers, and so I could not possibly ignore this lapse. I walked straight into the house and shouted 'Guard Commander!' at the top of my voice. My meaning must have been clear, because a subaltern appeared immediately with two N.C.O.s. I pointed to the sentry, who unaccountably had not moved from his slovenly attitude; he was disarmed on the spot and marched away.

Colonel Okuyama had him confined in a bamboo cage so constructed that he could neither stand upright in it nor lie down; he was fed like an animal through the bars. When I asked the colonel how long this punishment was to last, Miura translated his reply.

'We have sentenced him to a fortnight in the cage. But if you wish that we should execute the fellow, that can be done afterwards.'

'No,' I answered, suppressing a shudder. 'That will not be necessary.' But I had no authority to alter the sentence, and the poor man was still in his cage when I left for Surabaja.

The next morning, Friday, 1st March, passed in a fever of final preparations. Neville hurried off to the beach-head, while Shaw and I toured the whole area, inspecting troop dispositions and checking the billeting arrangements for the Dutch; the buildings of the Bali Hotel and its annex had been cleared to house, in addition to Colonel Ter Meulen and his staff, sixteen war correspondents of various nationalities who were arriving at the same time and who, we had been warned, would expect, and must receive, V.I.P. treatment.

We spent the latter part of the morning studying and collating the intelligence reports which poured in from the Rajahs and the Japanese garrisons in various parts of the island. Things seemed to be quiet everywhere, for the moment at least; I could only hope that they would remain quiet and that the gods of Bali, who had watched so many invasions in the past, would look kindly upon this one.

119

'I really don't think there's much more we could have done,' commented Shaw, 'in the very short time at our disposal. You realize, don't you, that we haven't been here a week yet?'

'It's incredible! I seem to have lost all track of time since we arrived—there've been so many other things to think about. Let's see, today's Friday, isn't it? You're quite right—it was only last Saturday that we anchored off Benoa and caught our first glimpse of Bali. It seems ages ago.

'I suppose everything will be all right tomorrow,' I continued doubtfully. 'But I'm not absolutely happy about Tabanan. After Den Pasar it's the worst area of the lot, and the Rajah is old, weak and scared.'

'I know, but you've got it pretty well sealed off by the Nips, haven't you? For heaven's sake stop fussing, Peter! Just relax for a change. You've been like a bloody old hen with chicks—flap, flap, flap! What about going to see Theo this afternoon?'

'Damned good idea. Can we get to Iseh and back before dinner?'

'Easily, now I know the way. We might do worse than take him one of our gallon jars of rum. We've got plenty here, and he'll certainly appreciate it. It'll probably save our own lives as well—otherwise we'll have to drink that lethal Swhisky.'

We reached Klungkung in the height of the afternoon and, turning left at the crossroads by the Kerta Gosa, began to climb into the foothills of Gunung Agung. After ten miles, at the sprawling, untidy village of Rendang, we turned to the right and travelled eastwards along a mountain road which soon dropped into a broad and fertile valley. On our left rose the mighty flank of Gunung Agung; on the right the paddy-fields stretched level to a line of low but steep and thickly wooded hills, among which we could see the lighter green of coconut plantations and the palm-thatch roofs of a few buildings.

'There,' said Shaw, 'is Iseh.'

We branched off to the right along a rough track across the fields towards the hills; as we approached, they seemed to rise sheer above us, the terraced ricefields meeting the rich green jungle where a wide path climbed at a gentle angle across the hill-side. We roared up the winding track, which came to an abrupt end in a tiny market-place among a few poor dwellings, little better than hovels; on our right the path led up the hill to a neat wooden house with a wide veranda.

From that direction, as we climbed out of the car, came a loud and cheerful greeting.

'Ho, ho, ho, *mon colonel*! I turned to see a figure in a striped singlet, dark blue shorts, and sandals running down the hill towards us with arms waving in welcome. 'Ho, ho, ho! Theo Meier makes you welcome to his house!' A moment later a dark, tubby little man with twinkling eyes and an enchanting mischievous smile was standing in front of us, vigorously shaking hands alternately with Shaw and me and patting Shimada on the shoulder, while a group of grinning villagers stood by, bowing and murmuring '*tabé, Tuan Besar!*' His merry eyes lit up when he saw us pull the wicker jar of rum from the car and start to carry it up the hill.

'Ho, ho, ho! *Ausgezeichnet!*' he chuckled. 'Now we drink together. *Patut, patut!* But first you try my Swhisky.' Shaw caught my eye and gave a faint shudder.

Theo Meier's home was almost a village in itself. In addition to the house there were several bales, or pavilions, for his servants and dependents, and one, containing a single room, for the exclusive use of his wife; there she would go to worship her household gods and there, so Meier told me, she would seclude herself from the sight of all men, including her husband, during the periods when she was *sebel*—unclean. The house was a fine, compact building of wood and brick, built by the artist himself with the help of the villagers; perched on the hillside between the ricefields and the jungle, it looked across the valley of Selat to the scrub-covered slopes and cloud-wrapped crater of Gunung Agung.

A flight of steps led from the path up to the veranda; at the top stood two of Meier's retainers, a slim, good-looking boy in a loin-cloth who saluted us with a cheerful grin, and an old man with a straggly, drooping moustache and a fringe of grey-flecked stubble round his chin, wearing a green robe. 'I call him the Monkey-Man,' said Meier, indicating the boy. 'When we go hunting the monkeys on the hill up there, to keep them from robbing the plantations, he is my shikar.' He chuckled to himself. 'He is fantastic, that one, at finding monkeys,' The other man was probably younger than he looked at first sight; but his slack, half-open lips and red-rimmed watery eyes indicated a constant and heavy drinker. He mouthed us a slobbery greeting, his shaven head bobbing up and down as he mumbled his words.

'He used to be a priest of Siwa,' Meier explained, 'at the temple of Besakih over there on Gunung Agung—the most holy temple in Bali. But, as you see, he is always drinking. He used to appear drunk at all the ceremonies and sacrifices, and so they sent him away. Now he lives here and is my very devoted friend.' The old man's face lit up in a fond and childish smile that was strangely moving.

From the shadow of the doorway three girls were watching; their ages ranged from about twenty-one to a bare thirteen. Gravely and gracefully they bowed us welcome, and then, at a sign from Meier, stepped forward each in turn. Shaw had not exaggerated: they were indeed beautiful.

'This is Madé Pegi, my wife.' Meier put an arm round the shoulder of the eldest. 'Now she only speaks Balinese and Malay, but soon we teach her to speak English, we three together.'

'Of course,' I answered. 'But first we must learn,' I broke off, staring in wonder at the beauty of this slender girl. Her dark eyes gazed steadily back at

121

me from an oval face beneath a smooth, broad forehead from which the hair was combed back in the shape of a high arch; a soft, shy smile curved the corners of her fine and sensitive mouth. In a gentle voice she murmured some words of Balinese, which Meier translated; but I scarcely heard him. I was conscious only of that exquisite face and slim figure and the swell of the young breasts beneath their covering of gold and crimson brocade. There seemed a certain wistfulness about her serenity but in those lovely eyes and delicate lips glowed a disturbing intensity of passion.

'And this is Njoman Pespes,' Meier's voice, faintly amused, brought me to my senses; with an effort I turned to smile back at a stocky but comely girl of fifteen or sixteen. 'Pespes,' he continued, 'means riches in Balinese. But her family, who live in Iseh, are very poor, and so she lives here and helps Madé Pegi.'

'Now this one,' he patted the youngest, 'we call Hungry Eyes.' She was a mischievous, slant-eyed urchin, as bright as a bee. 'She is living with us also, since six or eight months,' He lowered his voice confidentially, 'At first I would not permit myself to go to bed with her. But afterwards,' he grinned impishly, 'I find the Monkey-Man with her—*et alors*, she is no longer vierge!' He pinched the little girl's cheek; she answered with a little crow of laughter and a saucy wink.

We sat on benches at a long table while the girls fetched us glasses and bottles of Meier's home-distilled *arak*—'as drunk by the Swiss mountain sailors'—the labels assured us. Our host kept up an incessant flow of chatter, darting sharp glances at each of us in turn, his brown eyes flashing merrily and his head jerking from side to side like an agitated jackdaw. He raised his glass.

'*Selamat minum!* That is how you say "Cheerio!" in Malay. *Selamat minum, tuan besar!*' And he drained his glass.

I drained mine too, but I was unable to reply '*selamat minum*' or anything else for several minutes; my voice seemed to shrivel in my throat and my eyes were blinded with tears as I swallowed that dose of liquid fire. Not since I had been obliged to drink a mixture of raw alcohol and petrol with some friendly officers of a Russian armoured division in Poland had I administered such a painful shock to my system.

'*Tjumpol!*' he went on, fortunately without observing my distress. He smacked his lips appreciatively. "'*Tjumpol*' is *wunderbar* in high Balinese. You must learn these words. To say *tjumpol* or *patut*—very right—to these peoples makes great fun all over the place.' He picked up the jar of rum from the floor. 'Now we drink some of this. It is good you bring me the rum, it is more safe than *arak*. I like also the *arak*, you understand, but now since a few days I find *des jolis cristaux dorés dans mon pipi* and I must be prudent.'

'Herr Meier,' I began as soon as I could find my voice; but he cut me off.

'Oh no, *mon colonel*, please! You must call me Theo. Everybody in Bali is calling me Theo. It is many years since any man calls me Herr Meier. *Patut!* So now you call me Theo.'

'Where did you live before you came to Bali, Theo?'

'In the Marquesas.'

'I see. Like Gauguin.'

'Ah, Gauguin! Gauguin is my master—all I know of painting I learn from his work. Always I hope I paint like Gauguin.'

'And why did you leave the Marquesas?'

'I was not happy. The Marquesas is not like when is there Gauguin. And so I come to Bali, where is much better for me.'

'You came at once to Iseh?'

He shook his head. 'At first we live near Sanoer by the sea, my friend Schlager and I. Dr. Ernst Schlager, he is Director for the Orient of the Sandoz chemical *fabrik*; he comes from Basle like me. He has made the study of the Bali music and has transcribed it in European tones, and we both together make the study of the custom and religion; also we drink plenty *arak* and most—that is *tuak*—and make great fun all the time! Then Schlager is going to Switzerland, and I come here.'

'And you are happy here alone?'

He jerked his head towards the girls and smiled.

Our talk turned inevitably to the state of Bali. 'What did you mean,' I asked, 'when you wrote me that "freedom is not believed" here?'

He smiled. 'You know about lontars,'[1] Good. Well, in one important *lontar* is written, "It is fair to lie to wives and enemies." And so no Balinese man believe you when you promise freedom.'

'But why should they think of me as an enemy?'

'Why? Four years' miserable life, four years' first-class Japs' propaganda, and many serious patriots—not only the Bali-Nazi terrorists—created the *unum idea* that every foreign country is enemy as soon as they land.' He laughed shortly. 'Silly public idea is often fact more real than *verité!*'

'My friend Schlager and I find out that we are in front of a primitive people with *high culture* and *high standard* of life in its way. Moral don't exist here—not in our way of thinking. Don't speak to primitive peoples in abstract, logic way—they are never ready to be moved by it; but they are immediately moved by their way of thinking. Like this: you are Rajah, you are strong, you trust them, you don't make speeches, you can rule, you forbid *ribut*—violence, you are the *tuans*, you know everything!' His earnest little face relaxed in a wide grin.

---

[1] Ancient manuscripts, written on the leaves of the lontar palm, recording the history and literature of Hindu Java.

'I see,' I answered, not quite truthfully. 'But I have no authority to promise them freedom. My duty is simply to keep the peace.'

'Listen, please. You know what is *Eid-genossenschaft*? Well, Switzerland is a country with several different native populations living together as *Eid-genossenschaft*. Up to its present form was much organic development—through hundreds of years. It started small and was in time of seven hundred years enlarged. Religion and foreign wars unified us. Now Bali has never been a *Eid-genossenschaft*. Since always one county—one state—has fighted the others, and if for a certain time the *Dewa Agungs* kept most of it together, it was by *definite ungentle pressing*.' He ground his fist on the table. 'Yes, the Rajahs' power was merely on *takut* and rarely on *malu* based. The Holland government unified almost the land of Bali and the Japs kept on. But the chaotic structure of Balinese country has had not enough time of organic development towards peaceful understanding one the other. There are many—there are more as is ordinarily known—village-republics and sippen-verbände going criss-cross through Bali, and religious differences too.

'The greatest part of Bali is just now quiet—at least looked upon from far—but the organic joining together of the last thirty years is exhausted and needs immediate friendly kind help in administrative matters. This is the cause of the murders in Badung and Tabanan.'

'You mean,' I asked, somewhat confused by his efforts to explain a difficult problem in a language he had not spoken for at least four years, 'you mean that these murders are the result of personal or family feuds, not the work of political terrorists?'

'Terrorists? Yes, without doubt many of them are made by politic terrorists—*Bali-Nazis*, I call them. But many killings also are for *adat*,[1] because the breaking-up of organic unity.'

He sat back and swallowed a glass of rum. I was silent for a while. I understood what Shaw had meant when he described Theo's writing as rambling on like his conversation. Whatever the value of his opinion it was clearly too late for me to profit from it. But the Dutch might find it useful, and so I readily accepted his invitation to visit him again as soon as possible after the landings; I would bring with me his old friend, Daan Hubrecht.

Before leaving I asked Theo if there was anything we could bring or send him from Den Pasar. His own needs, he replied, were simple: canvases, paint and brushes. They would probably have to come from Singapore, but I promised to order them at once. However, he begged me to send him immediately a supply of medicines for the clinic which he held every morning in the village; he had virtually nothing to give his patients, who suffered, as far as I could gather, chiefly from skin complaints, gonorrhoea and trachoma; the last two were common sources of infection to the children's eyes.

---

[1] Village law and custom—a word adopted from the Arabic.

'When did you start this clinic?' I asked, wondering also where he had acquired his medical knowledge.

'My friend Schlager and I, we start it when we come here. Schlager is doctor of *pharnacopoea*. Also our good friend Dr. Hausman from Java has given us much help. From them,' he smiled proudly, 'I learn all my skill.'[1]

The entire household accompanied us to the car. We found Shimada chatting with a group of villagers armed with spears. 'These are my guards,' explained Theo. 'Some of them do the service every night to protect me from the Pemudas; so you see, I am quite safe here.'[2]

---

[1] According to Covarrubias (op. cit., p. 351), the Balinese have no faith in Western medicines, believing that they can only cure the people who invented them; they will only accept treatment out of politeness or when everything else has failed them. However, as I later saw for myself, Theo's 'clinic' was well attended by villagers, who seemed to hold him in great reverence as well as affection.

[2] But four years later even Theo had to flee from another outburst of anti-European terrorism.

X

THE LANDING

In the cool freshness of a brilliant morning I stood with Shaw and Neville on the beach-head, gazing seawards through my glasses at the two large landing-ships of the Royal Navy as they discharged through the gaping ports in their hulls a swarm of soldiers and equipment into the smaller craft that were to ferry them ashore; beyond I could make out the long, low silhouette of a Dutch destroyer. A mile to the west the sparkling blue sea creamed in breakers on the reef of the Sanoer lagoon, but here in the shallow little bay the waves lapped quietly along the stretch of shining sand.

Behind us, in the scrub-covered hinterland that separated the foreshore from the road, Japanese troops had been in position since the previous evening. Small groups of infantrymen crouched silently at action stations in the sandbagged weapon-pits that formed a wide semi-circle protecting the beach-head; others were posted in strategic positions all along the roads leading to Den Pasar. These military precautions that intruded so grimly on the lazy, colourful, sun-drenched landscape were a chilly reminder of the menace that lay hidden but still alert beneath the sensual tropical beauty of this enchanting island.

I looked around uneasily. The landing-craft had begun their run to the shore; the leaders, riding smoothly over the calm water, were already inside the bay. A few groups of villagers and fishermen watched the scene from a distance, but with curiosity rather than excitement, and certainly not with any evident hostility. Surely we had done everything conceivable to prevent bloodshed on this morning? At my side Shaw gave a gasp of surprise.

'Look who's here!'

Forgetting the traditions of Eton and the Royal Horse Guards he extended his arm to point at a couple of figures hurrying with short steps along the beach towards us; I recognized Polok's green sash and magenta kamben.

'What's brought you here?' I asked Le Mayeur when we had exchanged greetings. He pointed out to sea.

' When we saw those ships at sunrise I knew it must mean that the Allies were going to land. So we came along to watch. You do not mind?'

'On the contrary. My one fear has been that some trigger-happy Dutchman might loose off at one of those groups of Balinese and cause an incident. But now I can relax. The sight of your lovely Polok is just what we need to ease the tension.'

I turned to watch the first wave of the assault come in. The landing-craft ran on to the gently shelving beach; the ramps came down and the troops, in full battle order, splashed ashore; the operation was proceeding with the smooth precision of a well-run training exercise—which indeed was what it most resembled. The green-clad, steel-helmeted figures—tall, sun-tanned Dutchmen and lithe, dark-skinned Eurasians—swept forward up the beach, their faces set and grim, their bodies bent forward over their levelled tommy-guns. Then they caught sight of Polok, bright-clad, Junoesque and smiling. For a moment they paused. Their mouths sagged open in amazement; the barrels of their guns wavered uncertainly, and swung towards the ground; and then with a great cheer and flourish of hands they surged forward off the beach to their assembly points round the bridgehead.

I gave a great gasp of relief and turned to greet Colonel Ter Meulen, who was stepping ashore with his staff; with him was that amiable and distinguished soldier, Brigadier Geoffrey Bourne, C.R.A. to 5th Indian Division, who was accompanying the invasion force as observer on behalf of General Mansergh. From this moment Ter Meulen was in command on Bali, and I was only his adviser; I could almost feel the weight of responsibility roll from my shoulders as I shook his hand.

'Mission completed!' Shaw sighed happily and poured another round of rum sours. The three of us were sitting with Brigadier Bourne in my office at the Residency in the cool of the evening before dinner. We had reason to feel content. The entire Dutch force, consisting of two battalions and numbering some two and a half thousand men, had landed without incident and, for the moment at least, without encountering any sign of hostility; the Japanese had provided all the necessary transport and, as *The Times* correspondent wrote in his dispatch, 'by midday Dutch convoys were pouring into the interior taking over vital points from the Japanese, and the allied military administration was in control.'[1]

Even the journalists, who included such formidable American personalities as Martha Gellhorn and Bob Sherrard, seemed satisfied with our arrangements for their reception, although there was an indignant outburst from Miss Gellhorn when she was asked by the management of the Bali Hotel to share a room with an Eurasian girl; there was no other room available in the hotel, but I solved the problem by giving her my bedroom at the Residency, and moving my own bed into my office.

Now that the operation was over I could not help wondering why the Dutch had chosen to make an assault landing instead of coming ashore, as we had done, in the harbour at Benoa. When, long afterwards, I put this question to Colonel Carroll he chuckled.

---

[1] *The Times*, 4th March 1946.

'Nothing would convince them, up to the very last moment, that they weren't going to be opposed.'

'By whom? The Japanese or the locals?'

'The locals. It seems that Japanese propaganda had made its mark even on the Dutch High Command. You know, the landing-force had strict orders to withdraw on the first sign of opposition.'

'I notice,' observed the brigadier, 'that the people here have developed that odious Nip habit of bowing three times from the waist when we pass.'

'The Japanese taught them that,' I explained. 'We tried to stop it, but we couldn't in a week cure them of a habit they've learnt—and learnt the hard way—over a period of three years.'

'I suppose not. Let's hope the Dutch will put a stop to it. By the way, Ter Meulen seems most grateful to you all.'

'I only hope he feels the same way after a week or two.'

'You think they're going to have trouble, then?'

'I don't honestly know, sir. I believe that the great majority of Balinese don't want trouble. What they want above all else is peace and the chance to till their ricefields and follow their old, delightful, easy way of life without interference and without fear. But when have the great majority—especially in the East—ever been able to make their wishes felt against the determination of a ruthless, well-organized minority? As long as we were here on our own the terrorists were content to lie low and watch, confining their actions to a few carefully selected incidents in order to demonstrate their power—to show the flag, you might say. It's possible that if this force that landed today had been a British, or even an inter-Allied force, they might have remained comparatively quiet. But now they know the Dutch are back they may start serious guerrilla warfare—and the country's ideal for that.'

'You don't think they'll get much help from the mass of the population?'

'No, but they won't get much opposition either. Some of the population, I'm sure, really welcome back the Dutch; others are just indifferent. But all of them are much too frightened of the terrorists to give the Dutch any help, even if their Rajahs told them to—which they certainly won't in Den Pasar or Tabanan.'

'These terrorists, are they Balinese mostly, or Javanese?'

Shaw intervened. 'Numerically, they would be mostly Balinese, wouldn't they, Peter? But we're convinced that the inspiration, the leadership and the organization of the movement is Javanese; it is directed and controlled from Java—hence, of course, its lack of popular support.'

'Do you think the terrorists are getting any help from the Japs here?'

'We can find no evidence of it,' I said. 'Of course, they probably have informers among them, but we'll never know who they are.'

'How many Javanese would you estimate there are in Bali?'

'Only a few thousands, of whom about three hundred are active and dangerous; I'm talking of those in the towns and villages—I don't know how many there are with the gangs in the hills.'

'Oughtn't you to have done something about the dangerous ones?'

'We certainly ought—looking back on it now. We should have clamped down on them the moment we arrived. But we didn't have the information or the resources then; also, I wanted to avoid anything that might savour of repression. But now I'm convinced that one of the first things the Dutch should do is to round up those three hundred and either deport them to Java or keep them here under strict surveillance.'

The Brigadier laughed. 'Well, it's no longer your problem. You can talk to Ter Meulen about it in the morning.'

Although released from the pressure of the previous weeks, I had during the following days neither the opportunity nor the inclination to be idle. With Brigadier Bourne or with Sherrard and Miss Gellhorn we toured the island from Karangasem in the east to Djembrana in the west and northwards to Singaradja. I spent long hours in conference with Colonel Ter Meulen. Whether out of courtesy or because he really thought it useful, he sought my advice on almost every aspect of the political and military problem; and, to give us the benefit of that remarkable officer's ability and experience, he attached Daan Hubrecht to us for liaison duties between the two headquarters.

The day after the landing, 3rd March, we accompanied Ter Meulen to Klungkung for his first meeting with the Council of Rajahs. After a simple and informal lunch given by the *Dewa Agung* the business of the conference proceeded smoothly, without any of the tension of the previous meeting; the Rajahs pledged their full support to Ter Meulen, and he in return promised to reorganize and arm their police. In this atmosphere of friendliness and confidence some of my anxieties began to disperse.

This was the first day of the feast of *njepi*, marking the spring equinox, the end of the rainy season, and the Balinese New Year;[1] on this day every community in the island clears out its devils and evil spirits. 'It is believed,' says Covarrubias, 'that then the Lord of Hell, Yama, sweeps Hades of devils, which fall on Bali, making it imperative that the whole of the island be purified.' The festival lasts two days—the *metjaru*, the day of purification, and the *njepi* proper, the day of silence.

In Den Pasar that morning we had seen men carrying fighting cocks in their curious coconut baskets to the meeting halls for the cockfights which

---

[1] *Njepi* is the only festival of the old Hindu *saka* calendar still celebrated throughout this island; this calendar was superseded in Madjapahit times by the *wuku* calendar divided simply into weeks.

129

are an essential part of the celebrations; for the land is cleansed by the spilling of blood upon it. The purification rites take place before sunset, when the devils and evil spirits are lured to the *metjaru*—the 'great offering'—for the ceremony of expulsion; the *metjaru* is a strange assortment of objects laid out on the ground in the form of an eight-pointed star and surrounded by a low palm-leaf fence: there is every kind of food and strong drink, money and household utensils, samples of every seed and fruit growing on the island, and a piece of the flesh of every wild and domestic animal in Bali. A low-caste priest, the *sunguhu*, dedicates these offerings to the evil spirits, who converge all unsuspecting upon the sacrificial ground; once assembled there, they are expelled in a body by powerful *mantras* chanted by the waiting High Priests.

The populace take over the work where the priests leave off, and in Den Pasar we were treated to a noisy night. To the accompaniment of the furious throbbing of the *kulkuls* and the sharp explosions of firecrackers groups of men roamed the town carrying torches, beating drums, gongs, empty petrol tins, the ground and the trees, and shouting at the tops of their voices to frighten away any lurking devils, any *kalas* or *butas* that might have evaded the curses of the priests.[1]

In normal times the day of silence was most strictly enforced. No fires might be lit, for cooking or any other purpose—it was unlawful even to smoke a cigarette; there was no traffic on the roads; no work and no sexual intercourse were permitted on this day. Under present circumstances the last was the only prohibition we felt ourselves bound to observe; nevertheless we remained in Den Pasar, where there was plenty to keep us busy in conference and office.

On 5th March Brigadier Bourne flew back to Surabaja, taking off from the airstrip at Kuta which Shaw's Japanese working parties had made serviceable; he would return to Bali in three days' time with General Mansergh.

Den Pasar seemed to settle down peacefully enough under the new occupation. The townspeople, cautious at first, soon welcomed the Dutch troops, and shops and market-vendors did a brisk trade. Ter Meulen formed a defended perimeter around the town, with check points and road blocks covering all approaches; no European was allowed to wander outside without an escort. The terrorists had not yet shown their hand, but neither were they idle. Their first move was to impose a boycott on Den Pasar, and they were able to interfere seriously with the supply of food from the countryside; Ter Meulen soon found himself with a food shortage on his hands, and he had to call upon Surabaja for help.

---

[1] For a detailed description of this ceremony see *Island of Bali*, p. 279-282.

The focus of terrorist activity was Tabanan. Whatever the feelings of the Rajah, he was much too frightened of the terrorists to take any action against them, or even to ask Ter Meulen for protection. Murders continued on a large scale, so that no Balinese suspected of sympathy with the Dutch could consider his life safe; the civil administration had virtually collapsed. That this was an unfriendly district was made clear to Ter Meulen on his first visit. 'The attitude of the people along the roads towards us,' he wrote in his report, 'was mistrustful and without any sign of welcome.' And he concluded: 'The situation in Tabanan is most alarming.' It was not long before the trouble spread.

To divert ourselves from this depressing picture Shaw, Hubrecht and I drove up to Iseh to see Theo Meier, taking with us another jar of rum—and, on Ter Meulen's orders, a substantial escort. The little man was ecstatic to see his old friend again, and the beautiful Pegi shed tears of joy, exclaiming that now everything was going to be the same as it had been in the days before the war. When the time came for us to leave, Theo insisted on accompanying us back to Den Pasar; he wanted to see Van Burger, the new chief of civil administration, and give him advice on how to govern the island. I gladly offered to put him up.

'Ho, ho, ho!' he chorded as he skipped down the path to our jeep, while Pegi and the two girls waved us good-bye. 'Ho, ho, ho! Tonight we make the celebration in the headquarters of *mon colonel* Peter—the conqueror of Bali!' I prayed he would not talk like that to Van Burger.

We certainly made a celebration, and it was a noisy one, lasting late into the night; unfortunately it disturbed my other guest, whom in the excitement I had temporarily forgotten. Miss Gellhorn's furious protests broke in upon our revels, sobering me instantly as I remembered General Mansergh's strict instructions on the importance of the Press. Seeing my crestfallen expression Theo patted me reassuringly on the shoulder.

'Do not worry, Peter,' he whispered. 'Now I make everything all right with her.' He tiptoed across the room.

'Where are you going?' I asked anxiously.

He gave a devilish leer. 'I go to her now, and I make love to her. Yes?' And he padded through the door.

'Theo, come back at once!' I stopped him in his tracks with a voice of command I had not used since my arrival in Bali. 'I don't mind your getting your face slapped, but I'm not going to end my military career with a court martial.'

Shaw and I stood in silence on the quarterdeck of *Loch Eck* as she glided over the calm water towards the sunset. The previous day had seen the culmination of our work in Bali, when, at an impressive ceremony on the

Alun-Alun, General Mansergh had officially accepted the surrender of the Japanese garrison.

The next morning he had flown back to Surabaja with Brigadier Bourne; in the afternoon I had embarked my party in the frigate to follow them and prepare for our mission to Lombok.

Warmed by General Mansergh's praise and the effusive thanks of Ter Meulen and his officers, I had good reason to bless my luck; especially I blessed the two officers on my staff who had done most of the work for which I was getting the credit. But as I watched the land fade into the dusk astern I wondered uneasily whether our work there was going to prove so useful in the long run as it might seem at the moment; I was afraid Ter Meulen's stay in Bali would not be so peaceful as his landing.

Except for Surabaja the Indonesian nationalists held the whole of East Java; it was too easy for them to infiltrate arms and agents across the narrow waters of the Bali Strait. They had already shown that in Bali they had an organization efficient, cunning and ruthless enough to impose their will on large sections of the people, while the Dutch had nowhere near enough troops to winkle them out from that difficult, well-wooded, broken country. With foreboding I remembered the words spoken to me in Singaradja: 'Bali has been called "the last Paradise". Will it become the "*lost* Paradise"?'

XI

LOMBOK

Lombok is smaller than Bali, measuring some thirty miles from east to west and forty-five from north to south. The Lombok Strait dividing the two islands is one of the main waterways for shipping between South-East Asia and Australia; it holds some uncomfortable memories for Allied submariners of the Pacific War, who suffered much from Japanese patrols in its deep but narrow waters. It is also, according to the naturalist Wallace, the demarcation line between the flora and fauna of Asia, still found on Bali, and those of Australia, which begin to appear on Lombok; there have been various modifications of 'Wallace's line' during the ninety years since its promulgation, but Professor Dobby has noted that the drier climate of east Lombok has 'an almost Australian aspect, with prickly pears and cockatoos indicating the migration of Australian flora and fauna.'[1]

The north of the island is bare and mountainous; it rises steeply from the sea to the cloud-topped and still active crater of the great twelve thousand foot volcano, Rindjani, where, so the simpler islanders believe, dwells the spirit of the well-loved Lieftinck, first Dutch Resident of Lombok, forever keeping watch over his people. In the south is a barren limestone massif, about a thousand feet high, waterless and almost uninhabited, covered with scrub and bamboo thickets. Across the centre of the island, beneath the gentle southern slopes of the volcanoes Rindjani and Nangi, runs a fertile, well-watered and intensely cultivated belt of terraced ricefields and plantations, which produces enough food for the entire population of nearly a million.

Almost nine-tenths of this population are Sasaks, a simple agricultural people of Malay stock without the highly developed culture of the Balinese but with an infinite capacity for enjoyment and a remarkable aptitude for clowning. By religion they are what is called 'lax Moslems', and indeed Islam rests so lightly upon them as to be recognizable only in a few of their names. They are exceedingly promiscuous in their sex life, bringing to the pleasures of love a skill and enthusiasm unsurpassed by any people in my experience. Although given overmuch to robbery—but not to murder—they are an irresistibly lovable and friendly race, and they nurse remarkably little resentment for the wrongs they suffered under their former Balinese overlords.

---

[1] *South-East Asia*, University of London Press, 1950, p. 275.

The Balinese completed their conquest of Lombok in 1740, and for more than a century and a half a line of semi-independent Rajahs ruled the island from their fortress palaces at Mataran, the capital, and Tjakra Negara. In 1885 the Sasak chiefs rebelled and asked the Dutch for help against their Balinese governors; but it was not until 1894 that the Dutch sent an expeditionary force to occupy the island. After a bloody campaign, in which the invaders suffered one severe defeat, the Balinese fortresses were destroyed, Mataran was razed to the ground, and the old Rajah was sent to die of a broken heart in Batavia; the Dutch allowed his successors a limited jurisdiction over the forty thousand Balinese in Lombok, but they annexed the island and governed it through their Resident in Mataran. Friction between Balinese and Sasaks died down, although the Balinese, who remained in possession of the richest ricefields, naturally attracted some jealousy, especially from the old and impoverished Sasak nobility.

In addition to Sasaks and Balinese there is a small but commercially active Chinese community in the port of Ampenan, an Arab colony, and a few villages of Bugi traders.[1]

There was nothing complicated about the orders I received for this new operation; they ran as follows: 'You will land in Lombok to transmit latest military and political information and prepare for the landing of Dutch troops on Lombok.' But the written brief that accompanied them was far from reassuring. 'Japanese forces, totalling 409 Naval and 1945 Army personnel [sic] are concentrated in Mataran. They cannot be expected to control the civilian population in the event of a major disturbance, except in the immediate vicinity of Mataran. The Japanese garrison is in possession of only a limited amount of arms, left to them by an Australian surveillance party.'

It was explained to me in Surabaja that the Australian party had turned up some months previously from one of the islands farther east, disarmed the Japanese and sailed back whence they had come; they had acted on their own initiative and without authority. My brief concluded with the encouraging forecast that 'the landing may well be opposed by the local inhabitants, who are known to possess a number of weapons.'

To keep the peace, therefore, until the Dutch arrived I must rely on a virtually disarmed and almost certainly demoralized Japanese garrison, reinforced by General Ando and his two officers, and on my own formidable party, consisting of Shaw and Neville, Sergeant Hopkins, six signallers, one

---

[1] Natives of Celébes, the Buginese are stricter Moslems than either Sasaks or Javanese. 'The Bugis and Mascassaris,' says Professor Dobby, 'were historically one of the most active Muslim seafaring peoples of the Indies, acquiring a notoriety as pirates and slavers; they now rank as an inter-island trading people whose little sailing ships may be found anywhere between Singapore and Port Moresby.'

cook and my escort of one N.C.O. and five troopers of the Royal Berkshire Yeomanry. I had been obliged, reluctantly, to leave our Buffs behind in Surabaja; but this new escort, though all of them equally young, were all just as enthusiastic as their predecessors, and would, I was certain, give a good account of themselves in trouble.

'One thing's for sure,' I observed to my two officers as *Loch Eck* carried us across the smiling blue waters of the Lombok Strait towards the gleaming white houses of Ampenan. 'We don't repeat the mistake we made in Bali. One squeak out of any agitator, and he goes straight inside. Once we let trouble spread in this set-up we haven't a hope of controlling it.'

With this amiable resolution I stepped ashore on the little pier at Ampenan on the morning of 19th March, to receive the salute of a Japanese guard of honour and drive the four miles inland to my new headquarters in the Residency at Mataran, where servants and interpreters were already waiting.

Ampenan, though the principal port of Lombok, was too exposed to the westerly monsoon to be suitable for an assault landing; the Dutch had therefore decided to come ashore at the small, land-locked harbour of Lembar, about fifteen miles farther down the coast. I sent Neville there immediately with a Japanese working-party of two hundred and a strong armed guard; he seemed to enjoy himself, for the work of preparation was much simpler than at Sanoer, and the local inhabitants gave him an enthusiastic welcome.

After my ominous briefing I was agreeably surprised at the friendliness of the people of Mataran and Ampenan—Balinese and Sasaks alike. From the moment of our arrival, whenever we went out, groups would gather round us in the streets, calling out greetings in Malay and asking us whether we intended to remain; they seemed genuinely delighted to hear that we did. There were a few truculent shouts of '*Merdeka!*' from young men in European dress, but they were almost pathetic in their isolation.

On our first evening in Mataran the leaders of the Balinese, Sasaks and Eurasian communities presented themselves in turn at the Residency to offer us their support.[1] The Balinese warned us to be very careful of the Sasak leader; the Sasaks advised us to have no dealings with the Balinese. The Eurasian urged us to trust no one. They were followed by an urbane and well-groomed Chinaman bearing an invitation to dinner with the Chinese Association of Ampanan; he gave us no advice or promises of support, but wished to present me with a typewriter—purely, of course, as a token of esteem.

---

[1] The Balinese representative was not Rajah, but an official in charge of the Balinese civil administration.

We enlisted the Eurasian as an extra interpreter, for besides excellent English he spoke Dutch, Malay, Balinese and Sasak. He was a soft-voiced, desiccated man in late middle age, with thin, silvery hair, a pronouncedly European cast of features and a melancholy, timorous expression; with his emaciated body, lean, sad face, and long, scrawny, undulating neck he reminded me of some weary and disillusioned old vulture. He had been a senior police official under the Dutch and his name was Mr. Smith.

Despite their suspicion of each other, Smith and the Balinese and Sasak leaders all agreed that there was on the island a small but potentially dangerous movement, under Javanese leadership, pledged to resist occupation by the Allies; they assured me that it had little support among the population, whose interest was in farming rather than politics, but they hinted that the Japanese were giving it clandestine help. Moreover, the day before our arrival a certain Kumenit, an agitator from Manado in north Celébes, had addressed a public meeting in Mataran, exhorting the people to 'oppose the Allies to the last drop of their blood.' There had also been some attempts at intimidation, but as yet no kidnapping or murder. I decided on an immediate show-down, to dispose of the malcontents and at the same time test the loyalty of the Japanese garrison.

I recognized my cue the following afternoon, when a party of four young Javanese presented themselves at the Residency and demanded an immediate interview in the name of the "National Independence Committee,' Their leader, I afterwards learned, was a clerk in a government office; the other three were schoolmasters. Trooping into my office they brusquely declined my invitation to sit down, and stood stiffly in front of my desk glaring at me with an angry self-assurance. Smith, looking more than usually woebegone and frightened, acted as interpreter. They wasted no time on courtesies.

'We have come,' declared their leader haughtily, 'to lay before you the people's demands for the civil administration of Lombok.'

I asked mildly by what right they, who were Javanese, claimed to speak for the people of Lombok. Quite unabashed he replied simply, 'We have been appointed.' He then launched into a fierce indictment of the Allies for their 'repression' in Java; demanded my assurance that the Dutch would not land in Lombok, and concluded by ordering me to hand over the civil administration immediately to his committee and confine myself to getting rid of the Japanese. His companions hung on his words with rapt attention, nodding their heads eagerly as he made each point.

Controlling my temper I heard him out to the end; then I stood up and coldly invited them to leave. It would be impolitic, as well as unethical, to detain them while they were technically my guests in the Residency; but that evening I told the Japanese to arrest their leader. I gave the same orders about his treatment and privileges as I had given for my prisoners in Bali. Two days later I visited him in prison and found him in excellent spirits; he seemed amused when I apologized for having to curtail his liberty, and clearly bore me no ill will. Shorn of his arrogance he seemed a delightful fellow.

I made the Japanese give me a copy in translation of their prison records, stating the name of each prisoner and the charge on which he was being held. I observed that in several cases the charge was listed simply as 'fornication'. After consultation with Balinese and Sasak officials I ordered the release of these men. 'I should feel extremely uncomfortable,' I explained to Shaw, 'to be holding anybody in gaol for that particular offence. Besides, even if it is a crime under Moslem law, it certainly isn't under Balinese or Sasak custom.'

Touring the island with Smith and the Sasak and Balinese leaders, Shaw and I interviewed the principal officials and head-men of every district, and soon had a clear picture of the situation. It was a great deal better than in Bali. From the information we collected I was able to identify the most dangerous characters; within four days I had ordered some thirty arrests, including three officers of the Japanese *Kempeitai*, one of them a war criminal and the other two *agents provocateurs* who had busied themselves in stirring up trouble between the Balinese and Sasaks.

With these arrests all sign of opposition ceased; it was quickly evident, in the cheerful faces of the people and the enthusiastic welcomes we received wherever we went, that a new and happier atmosphere prevailed in the island. Every day the Residency was thronged with deputations of villagers and headmen, come to declare their loyalty; they brought presents of pigs, ducks, eggs and *brom*, a potent wine made from black or red rice. The live-stock was something of an embarrassment, for their numbers threatened to overcrowd the small Residency compound; yet we could not hurt the feelings of our visitors by refusing their gifts. Sergeant Hopkins, whose medical duties were fortunately light, appointed himself chief swineherd, but we had to leave most of his charges to our Dutch successors.

The Japanese at first were slow to co-operate, especially in carrying out the arrests I ordered; we soon traced the fault to the attitude of their commander. He was an elderly colonel of slovenly manner and untidy appearance, whose attitude in our presence was a studied blend of apathy and insolence; at conferences he would sit sprawled in his chair with his jacket unbuttoned and his hands in his pockets, staring at the ceiling and occasionally yawning, and he carried out our instructions—when he carried them out at all—with unconcealed reluctance and ill grace. It was probably *ennui* that was affecting him rather than malice, but I could not afford to make allowances; and so I relieved him of his command and sent him under close arrest to Bali. We had no trouble from his successor.

Although we had less cause to worry now than when we were in Bali, we still had an extremely heavy load of work, and neither Shaw nor I had much time to sleep or to relax and enjoy the exuberant loveliness of this gaily coloured landscape. In addition to our daily tours of inspection, which took us all over the island, Shaw was busy with his old problem of Japanese troop concentrations to protect the Dutch landing at Lembar—for we dared not neglect any precautions—and the preparation of a landing-strip for aircraft on the east coast; while I was absorbed in a host of minor but still important matters—questions of civil administration, local law and custom, and village economy that were far outside my capacity or experience. Acting on the principle that it is better to give a wrong decision than none at all, I almost certainly gave a lot of wrong decisions.

On the morning of 27th March Colonel Ter Meulen led his troops ashore at Lembar, to be greeted by a crowd of cheering villagers; he brought with him his own motor transport, and by noon had occupied the capital. Mataram and Ampenan—indeed every village on the route from Lembar—came out in a rash of Dutch flags, which must have been concealed since before the war; the warmth and enthusiasm of the people's welcome far exceeded our brightest hopes. Indeed Brigadier Bourne, who once again accompanied Ter Meulen, signalled to General Mansergh: 'People's welcome both spontaneous and vociferous. Those who saw welcome to British in Malaya compare it equally.'

'That briefing we had in Surabaja,' I remarked to Shaw, 'was the most inaccurate appreciation of a situation I've ever come across.' We were standing outside the Residency with Ter Meulen and Jacobs, the new Dutch Resident, watching the happy, excited crowds that thronged the long, wide main street.

'It wouldn't have been,' he answered, 'if we hadn't learnt our lesson in Bali and muzzled the opposition here right away.'

'What will you do with them?' I asked Ter Meulen.

He shrugged his shoulders. 'Nothing. They will have to stay in prison until everything is normal here. Then they will be allowed to leave.'

The next morning, at an assembly of all the heads of district, the Balinese *pungawas*, the Sasak chiefs and the principal village headmen, Ter Meulen and Jacobs formally announced the return of Lombok to the Dutch Crown. At the end of the ceremony there were prolonged cheers, led by the Dutch but echoed enthusiastically by the people, for Queen Wilhelmina. The British and Dutch flags were hoisted over the Residency.

In the afternoon we watched a remarkable display of Sasak games on the great open space where the assembly had taken place in the morning. It consisted chiefly of a series of mock combats between two men armed with long, pliant rattan rods and wooden shields. Naked, save for their girded loincloths, the combatants pranced warily round each other, their shields raised over their heads, their right arms extended, trailing the rattans on the ground behind them; suddenly one of them would leap forward, swinging his staff in a high arc over the opposing shield at his adversary's head, or in a wide sweep round the shield at his ribs. Usually the shields parried these murderous blows, and nobody was hit on the head, but sometimes a sideways swipe would land with a sickening whack, loud as the impact of a bullet, on a man's bare ribs. When this happened there was a brief lull; the striker would execute a small dance of triumph in the middle of the arena, while his victim capered round the ring of spectators, grimacing horribly, pointing to the rapidly swelling weal on his flank and in turn giggling, crying with pain and shouting to his friends to admire his pluck. When they had finished their clowning they would resume the battle. The victims seemed to get more applause than the victors—but no shred of sympathy—from the delighted crowd; I never saw a man show the least sign of temper, although some of the bruises almost turned my stomach and the pain must have been excruciating.[1]

By contrast with this virile spectacle the dance we gave in the Residency that night for the Dutch officers and nurses was a pallid affair; but Shaw and I had no longer any worries to inhibit our enjoyment, and the fifteen gallons of 'operational' rum which 5th Indian Division had given us for this operation, and which we had scarcely broached since our arrival, proved an ideal lubricant. The Chinese Association had provided us with the elements of an orchestra; in the manner of Chinese merchants all the world over, they had dug up out of nowhere a piano, a trumpet and drums. The piano was a little out of tune, but so also was the pianist—Brigadier Bourne's soldier servant, who had learnt by correspondence course during his service in the Far East; a Dutchman played the trumpet, and the drummer was a Japanese sailor, who in peacetime had been the champion tap dancer of Tokyo.

At Ter Meulen's request we remained another week on Lombok, although there was very little for us to do. There was no serious opposition to the Dutch, and it seemed unlikely now that any would develop. The people, the Sasaks especially, were well disposed towards them; moreover, the island was not suitable for guerrilla warfare, for the cultivated area was too small, the mountains too bare and desolate to shelter bands of terrorists. Ter Meulen decided to hand over to Jacobs and return to the much more serious problems of Bali. On General Mansergh's orders I sent my party back to Surabaja, but Shaw and I, who had been granted a week's leave in Bali, left with Ter Meulen in an M.T.B. on 3rd April.

One of my last actions in Lombok was to make a farewell call on the Balinese Rajah in his palace. He welcomed me with warmth, remarking that I had come at a most auspicious moment; although seventy-five years old, he had that day been presented with a son by his youngest wife, a girl of

---

[1] These contests are very similar to the *Gebug* or *Endé*, performed as a dance in certain districts of East Bali (see *Dance and Drama in Bali*, pp. 265-7).

seventeen. To mark the occasion he gave me a fine *kolok* with a beautifully worked wooden sheath.

'I can't imagine what he thinks *you* had to do with it,' grumbled Shaw.

XII

AND FAREWELL GOES OUT SIGHING

Shaw and I had agreed with the Le Mayeurs and Theo to divide our leave between them; while he was staying with one I should stay with the others, and we should change round after three days. And so, when we landed at Karangasem on 3rd April Shaw took the road to Iseh, while I went straight to Sanoer, to the bamboo house beside the murmuring sea, and exchanged my uniform for a *kamben*, and slept a great deal, and bathed in the lagoon before breakfast, and lounged on the veranda watching the bright hibiscus in the garden glowing in the early morning sunshine, and listened to the sea breeze whispering in the tall sugar palms.

And yet I was not happy, for all the kindness of Le Mayeur and Polok. For the first time, almost, since I had dropped into Siam I had no responsibilities or urgent problems; I had plenty of time to think, and my thoughts were heavy and full of misery and self-reproach. In Lombok I had received a letter telling me that my wife had remarried. There I had been too busy—or I could make myself too busy—to think about it; but now I felt the full pain and desolation—mixed, let me be honest, with a large dose of hurt pride—of this news which I ought to have expected but somehow had never foreseen. Bitterly I cursed the selfishness and obstinate determination to go my own way that had wrecked my marriage and destroyed our love. And so I took no pleasure in this paradise, but brooded in a deep pit of loneliness and despair, and abused my fate, and hated myself, and wept a little, and drank too much, and wept some more.

This discreditable exhibition of *Angst und Schaden* was aggravated, though I did not recognize them at the time, by the early symptoms of the tuberculosis which eighteen months later almost ended my life. Apart from the usual persistent cough, to which I paid no attention, I became noticeably neurotic, short tempered and snappy, with spells of overpowering lassitude that seemed to deprive me of all my energy and will. At the time I put everything down to war-weariness and alcohol.

Ter Meulen, too, had his troubles, more serious than mine. On my way to Sanoer I had called at the hospital in Den Pasar to visit Van Burger, the Resident, who was lying in bed with a bullet wound in his stomach; terrorists had fired on his jeep as he was driving back from Singaradja. Luckily the wound was not dangerous, but this attack proved to be the first of many; emboldened by early success and the inability of the Dutch to retaliate, the

141

terrorists embarked on more ambitious operations, until they were ambushing troop convoys on the road to Tabanan.

On the 5th I took my leave of the Le Mayeurs and drove up into the cool green hills of Iseh. I arrived in the early evening, and all of a sudden my heart lifted at the welcoming light in Madé Pegi's lovely eyes. Theo and Shaw had gone to shoot monkeys in the plantations above the house; they came back just before dark with the Monkey-Man carrying five or six pathetic little furry bodies slung on a pole over his shoulder.

'I can't say I enjoy shooting them,' Shaw told me as he cleaned his carbine. 'It's too like shooting human beings, and they give a terribly human scream when they're hit.'

We had brought Theo another two gallons of rum—for our own sakes as much as his—and now, while he went to prepare our food, we lingered over our drinks on the porch, watching the deepening darkness spread from the valley up the lower slopes of Gunung Agung. Theo was a superb cook and was happy to spend hours in the kitchen, applying to his work a rare skill and a fine inventive flair; his specialty was *bifstek tartare*, which he would let no one make but himself—'for here in Bali,' he warned us, 'you can easily have some worm.' That night he gave us a curry which still lives in my memory, and not only for its flavour; when we asked him what was this delicious and tender meat, he smiled softly at Shaw.

'You have just shot them.'

The Dutch had lent us each a staff car, and so when Shaw left for Sanur I drove with Theo to visit the curious village-republic of Tenganan in the hills south-west of Karangasem. This is the most conservative of the Bali Aga communities, pure descendants of the ancient Indonesians who colonized the islands nearly two thousand years ago. Socially and economically it is entirely cut off from the rest of Bali, and its physical isolation is emphasized by a solid wall surrounding the village, pierced only by four very narrow gates; the life and customs of these Bali Aga have remained untouched by the religion and culture of the later Hindu Javanese conquerors.

The people of Tenganan are fair-skinned, with slender, fragile bodies, small bones, and the carefully cultivated, artificial manners of an effete and over-leisured aristocracy; they look down on other Balinese, and are themselves forbidden, on pain of exile, to marry outside the community. Their village is ruled by a council of Elders, who are also priests, and they worship the spirits of nature and of their ancestors. Their society is a form of patriarchal Communism, for they do not recognize the individual ownership of property; even the houses are all built alike, intersected in an austere, geometrical pattern by long straight avenues paved with stone. On the other hand, they are not permitted to work the rich and extensive ricefields and plantations owned by the village, but hire Balinese from outside as labourers.

142

As an indication of their superiority to manual work they grow their fingernails to an extraordinary length, those of the *perbekel*, or headman, who received us measuring at least four inches.

Strangers are not usually welcome in Tenganan, and we owed our invitation to Theo's friendship with the *perbekel*, a faded ghost of a man in his middle thirties who greeted us with formal courtesy and an air of well-bred languor. After he had escorted us through the village we sat down to sample a delicious fresh tuak from the local plantations—the preparation of this drink is the only agricultural labour the villagers allow themselves; Theo pointed out to me an old man who hovered in the background with a watchful, anxious expression.

'It is that one's duty,' he whispered, 'to sweep the village after we have gone, to brush away our footprints.'

In the clear, sweet air of Iseh, cooled by the dry wind that blew steadily from the east to fan those lush green hills and ricefields, my lethargy and my cares dissolved. Nobody, indeed, could remain gloomy for long in the company of Theo, with his bubbling vitality and lust for life, his warm humanity, and his bright and bawdy wit. Usually I saw more of Madé Pegi during the daytime than of Theo. During the morning, when he had finished with his clinic, he would retire to one of the hales to paint; in the afternoon he would visit a neighbouring village where the pungawa or pedanda was his friend, to return in the evening, breathless and flushed with excitement, followed by a retinue of servants staggering under the weight of heavy bamboo jars.

'Ho, ho, ho!' he would shout. '*Venez, venez,* Peter! *J'ai trouvé un* EXCELLENT *tuak! Nous allons goûter de ça!*'

Later, after we had eaten, we would sit with the girls on the terrace in the still, cool darkness, rich with the scent of frangipani and champaka, drinking tuak and talking while the full moon threw dappled shadows among the ricefields in the valley and bathed the slopes of Gunung Agung in grey and silver light. As the hours wore on the girls crept silently to bed; but I remained listening to Theo's stories of Bali and the Marquesas, till the darkness paled and dawn revealed the great mountain rising from the valley mists, its flattened cone outlined against a pearly sky.

One day we had a visit from a fellow-countryman of Theo's who had known him in Bali before the war; his name was Andoregg and he was working for the International Red Cross. Short and slight of build, with humorous eyes blinking behind thick horn-rimmed spectacles and a slow, hesitant manner of speech, he had the appearance of a benevolent but emaciated tortoise. He spoke good Malay and was popular among the Balinese, with whom he believed himself to have some special affinity; it was over-confidence in this belief that was to lead him to a terrible end.

Theo confessed to me that his married life had not always been easy. Madé Pegi was his second wife, and both she and her predecessor came from Sanoer, a village famous for the power of its priests and witch-doctors and the hysterical temperament of its women. He had kidnapped Madé Pegi, following the established Balinese custom, and for a while had lived with the two girls in his house by the sea. But his first wife had resented the intrusion, and her persistent jealousy had broken up his comfortable ménage; after she had made several skilful attempts to poison him and Madé Pegi he had felt obliged to send her away. She had gone to live in Den Pasar and Theo had brought Madé Pegi to Iseh. Although not actively inclined to homicide Madé Pegi was also capable, so Theo told me, of extravagant outbursts of indignation and he bore many bruises as evidence of the strength of her displeasure.

'You would not credit it, *mon cher*,' he assured me with wistful admiration, 'the force with which that little girl strike me.'

'She has the appearance of a passionate nature. But Theo,' I added impulsively, 'I have never seen a more beautiful girl and she is so wonderfully sweet to me!'

'Oh, yes,' he murmured with a sly grin. 'She is quite in love with you.' He giggled and wagged a finger in my face. 'Mais prenez garde, mon vieux! Je suis devenu amoureux de ma femme. Elle n'est plus couchable avec!'

Our leave was up on 10th April, but when I arrived in Den Pasar I was greeted with a request to report to Colonel Ter Meulen. Beneath his usual courteous manner I could see that he was very worried. A certain Colonel Tweedy, a British officer on the staff of A.F.N.E.I. who was spending his leave in Bali, had disappeared. He had wandered off on his own, most unwisely, to take photographs in a village north of Den Pasar; that was four days ago, and he had not been seen since. Ter Meulen suggested that Shaw and I might like to remain in Bali to help with the search; we readily agreed, and General Mansergh immediately signalled his approval.

We persuaded Ter Meulen to let Hubrecht join our party, and to lend us a jeep, together with our old chauffeur, Shimada. Hubrecht brought with him a Eurasian lieutenant, Jack Hagemann, one of the keenest and most efficient young officers I ever met, who spoke not only Dutch and English but perfect Malay—I never knew how beautiful a language Malay could be until I heard Hagemann speak it.

Our search for Colonel Tweedy developed into a search for leading terrorists or terrorist sympathizers who might know something about the murder—that he had been murdered there was little doubt. We obtained from the Dutch, from Theo and the Leo Mayeurs, and from our Balinese contacts the names of suspects or possible informants in the area between Den Pasar, Tabanan, Bangli and Gianjar, and these we set out to find and interrogate; we operated principally by night, partly because we could hope to surprise them sleeping, partly because at such a time they would show less resistance to questioning, but partly, I am sorry to admit, in the belief—naive and childish as it now seems—that our sudden appearance in a hostile area in the dead of night would have a profound effect on the morale of the terrorists.

We ran into trouble on the first evening. Driving back from Kesiman, where we had been questioning the *pungawa*—an old man high on our list of suspects who pleaded ignorance to all our questions—we came upon a large tree felled across the road; as we slowed down a heavy machine-gun opened fire on us from a plantation on the outskirts of Den Pasar. Fortunately the aim was high, and we were able to remove the road block and drive on, without lights, until we met a Dutch picket; they too had heard the firing, but by the time they had arrived on the scene the enemy had vanished.

We patrolled the whole area systematically, planning each operation carefully beforehand on our maps. We would drive to a point near our objective and walk the rest of the way, leaving Shimada, with a heavy service revolver in his hand and a broad, happy grin on his face, to guard the jeep. I had the greatest admiration for his courage when I thought of him standing there alone for two hours or more in the silent, hostile darkness; but someone had to stand guard, and Shimada begged so insistently to come on every operation that we hadn't the heart to leave him in Den Pasar. I am thankful that he came to no harm.

I felt pretty scared myself as we padded silently through the night along narrow paths through thick undergrowth, or among the tall, black trunks of palm trees that looked cold and evil and menacing in the pale light of the moon; by nature a timid person I imagined an army of dangers, real or ghostly, lurking in the surrounding darkness, and I would halt suddenly, gripping my carbine in a sweat of terror, ready to shoot at some shadow that I thought had moved.

I cannot pretend that we met with much success. The few suspects we caught either knew or would tell us nothing; but usually they had vanished before we arrived. The countryside was broken up into deep, narrow ravines between perpendicular walls of rock, overgrown with vegetation, where even in daylight fifty men might hide while we passed within a few feet. Once or twice, indeed, we had an encounter with a terrorist outpost or patrol—a brief, wild exchange of shots, the quick shadow of a running figure, and then silence in the empty night.

Looking back on it now, it all seems a most amateur, schoolboy performance and an irresponsible risk out of all proportion to anything we could hope to gain. The wonder is that we never met serious trouble; we must have been so easy to ambush. Years later some of the terrorist leaders told Hubrecht that on many occasions they had watched us and sometimes they had had us in their sights. Why they made no attempt to kill us all is something I can only attribute to Hubrecht's personal popularity with the Balinese, and to the well-known Oriental affection for lunatics and children.

After two weeks Shaw was summoned to Singapore, where a new post awaited him in SEAC, and early in May I received orders to report to General Mansergh, now Commander-in-Chief A.F.N.E.I., in Batavia. Tweedy's murderer was caught by the Dutch military police, trying to dispose of the poor man's watch. The motive of the murder was not political after all; it was plain robbery. Tweedy was carrying the three possessions most coveted by a Balinese: a watch, a camera, and a pistol; it was for these he was killed. The murderer, a man with a bad criminal record, stalked him and struck him down from behind; then he rolled the body into an irrigation ditch about a kilometre north of Den Pasar, cut off the flow of water with an improvised dam of earth, covered the body with stones, and let the water flow over it again. If there were any witnesses they never talked; it was the watch that gave the criminal away.

This murder led indirectly to another tragedy. Theo's friend Andoregg, who had visited us at Iseh, decided to look for Tweedy on his own. Trusting in his knowledge of the Balinese and in their affection for him, and disregarding all the warnings and entreaties of Ter Meulen, Hubrecht and even Theo himself, he put on Balinese dress and set off on foot alone into the countryside. He wandered from village to village, staying at night with the various *pungawas* and headmen whom he knew, and following any leads they could give him; every two or three days he would turn up in Den Pasar to report. Then he too vanished; for ten days nothing was heard of him. By that time I was in Java, and I was on the point of returning to Bali to look for him when news arrived that he had been found by a Dutch patrol: he was lying dead in a ricefield with a rope round his neck and more than thirty sword slashes in his poor mutilated body. I shuddered to think how very easily his fate might have been our own.

Lying on my stomach in the perspex nose of a Mitchell bomber, I shaded my eyes from the full glare of the declining sun and peered down to let them linger for the last time upon the lovely island dropping away beneath me as the aircraft straightened on her course towards Java. I was ashamed to feel the prickle of tears against my eyelids, and suddenly I could no longer stifle my sobs. On the airfield at Kuta, in front of Theo and Pegi, the Le Mayeurs and Hubrecht, I had just been able to control my feelings—although the sight of Shimada standing a little way behind the others with the tears streaming freely down his ugly face brought a sudden shock of pity and surprise; he must have enjoyed himself with us more than I had realized, and now he would have no more fun. But when I came to say good-bye to Madé Pegi I could scarcely hide my misery; I felt her trembling, too, as she kissed me. Theo put his hand gently on my own.

'You will come back to us,' he said. The others echoed his words, but I could not believe them. I felt I should never again find the peace and happiness I had experienced in that house among the bright green hills of Iseh, or be able to forget the moonlight on the slopes of Gunung Agung above the shadowed, silent valley.

I stayed only twenty-four hours in Surabaja, where I found the atmosphere less hospitable than before. This was due to the recent arrival of two Dutch marine brigades who had just completed their training in the United States; they were ill-disciplined, truculent and trigger-happy, and nursed against the British, whom by some curious process of reasoning they seemed to hold responsible for the collapse of their empire, a resentment scarcely less violent than their hatred of the Javanese. The following evening at dusk I landed at Batavia, and was driven straight to the Hotel des Indes, where some kindly Staff Officer had booked me a suite.

The standard of luxury for which this hotel was once so justly famous had, as I have already remarked, deteriorated since the war; one symptom of its decline became immediately clear to me on arrival, when I opened the door of my sitting-room, switched on the light and started to carry my luggage through to the bedroom. Half-way across the room I was arrested by the sound of agitated scuffling and, turning my eyes to the wall on my right, I saw a large brass-posted bed draped with a mosquito curtain suspended from the ceiling; the bed was shaking violently, from behind the curtain came the sound of heavy breathing, and dimly through the gauze I discerned the outline of a struggling figure.

I dropped my bags and stared in open-mouthed, speechless amazement as the curtain parted and there emerged not one but two figures, both of them as naked as—though in every detail more striking than—on the day they were born. The man was broadly built, with thick, short arms; he was deeply tanned and covered all over with black, curly hair. The girl was a young giantess, a round, vacant, pink and white doll's face on the smooth, glistening body of a whale; after ten years of war I was no longer squeamish, but my stomach fairly heaved when I glanced at those huge suety thighs.

'Well, hello!' called the man in a hearty, nasal voice. 'Come right in.' He fished out a pack of Lucky Strike from the pocket of a uniform jacket hanging on a chair by the bed; I noticed the four rings of a captain of the mercantile marine. He put a cigarette between the girl's fat lips, took another himself and threw one to me. 'Got a light?'

They sat side by side on the bed, smoking quietly and looking me over with a friendly curiosity while I struggled with my voice. At last in desperation I snatched a flask of whisky from my rucksack and passed it to them; then I took a long, deep pull myself. Never had I so badly needed a drink.

'Oh boy!' sighed the captain ecstatically. 'That was real Scotch!' Then he appeared to remember his manners. 'Gee, I'm sorry!' he apologized. 'I never introduced you.' He laid an enormous hand on the girl's bare shoulder. 'Honey, meet Colonel. . .'

'Kemp. Peter Kemp.' I bowed awkwardly, for I was still badly shaken. He heaved himself to his feet and shambled towards me, stretching out a hairy arm and beaming like some friendly forest gorilla.

'Hiya, Pete! This is just great! Now you call me Mike, see?'

I looked down at my dirty, sweat-sodden bush shirt and slacks, and came out with probably the silliest sentence of my life. 'I'm most terribly sorry,' I began, 'to be looking so untidy. You see, I've been travelling all day. . . .' I dived for the shelter of my bedroom.

A few minutes later, as I was about to take a shower, the captain appeared in the doorway. 'Mind if I come in?' He didn't wait for my answer; as he had put on a few clothes our positions were now reversed. He lowered his voice to a hoarse whisper. 'See here, Pete, Greta and me we've been havin' a little talk about you, and she thinks you're swell. Now I'm sailin' tomorrow, see, so why don't you kinda take over from me, see what I mean? She's a great girl,' he added with unconscious humour.

'Well now, Mike, that's awfully kind of you,' I began, hoping my face wouldn't betray the mounting horror inside me. 'But-'

'Aw, hell!' I winced as he slapped me on my unprotected back. 'You don't need to thank me, Pete. We're all pals out here. You'd do the same for me. She'll be at one of those tables out front of the hotel after lunch tomorrow, and she'll be lookin' for you.'

'Thanks for the tip, Mike,' I said with deep feeling.

'O.K., Pete. Bye now. Greta and me we're for another shack down.'

In order to escape I arranged to fly up to Bandaung, about a hundred miles inland, as the guest of an Indian Cavalry regiment. In this cool and picturesque mountain resort, surrounded by my genial and hospitable friends, I felt safe. Bandaung, held by 23rd Indian Division, was invested on all sides by hostile Indonesians, and the only safe approach to it from Batavia was by air; several convoys had been ambushed on the road with very heavy casualties. The Indonesians made no attempt to attack, at least while I was there, but there was a good deal of sniping in the town and it paid to be wary. Social life, however, was brisk, beginning after sundown and continuing, despite the curfew, late into the night. Even a sharp attack of gastritis, probably alcoholic, did little to spoil my pleasure.

Returning to Batavia a week later I learned that I was at last to go home; the War Office had written to A.F.N.E.I. pointing out that I was well overdue for demobilization. I reported for the last time to General Mansergh, who greeted me with his usual warmth and kindness.

'You've earned an air passage,' he said at the end of the interview. 'I'll sign an order now to give you priority.'

On 15th June I took off from Batavia for Singapore, on the first stage of my homeward journey. As the Dakota circled low over the city and turned out to sea across the harbour I gazed back sadly on my last view of Java. I knew I was bewitched forever by the strange, sultry beauty of those islands, and I felt a deep and painful longing for Bali and Lombok, for the charm of their people and the easy peace of their life—above all for the gaiety and kindness of Pegi and Theo and my friends at Sanoer. Europe, I thought, will seem a drab place after all this colour. It occurred to me now that I was just two months short of my thirty-first birthday and for ten years I had been almost continuously at war; I wondered how I should make out in peace.

ABOUT THE AUTHOR

Peter Kemp was an English soldier and writer. Educated at Wellington College and Trinity College in Cambridge, Kemp was preparing for a career as a lawyer before, alarmed by the spread of Communism, he volunteered to assist the Nationalists during the Spanish Civil War. Kemp saw extensive combat in both the Requetés militia and later the Spanish Foreign Legion. After the Civil War ended, Kemp was recruited as an agent for the British Special Operations Executive, taking part in numerous commando raids and other irregular warfare activities in France, Albania, Poland, and several colonial territories throughout the Pacific during and after the Second World War. His adventures are recorded in the books *Mine Were of* Trouble, *No Colours or Crest,* and *Alms for Oblivion.* After that war ended, he worked as an insurance salesman and international journalist, continuing his life of distinction and courage. He passed away on October 30, 1993.

Printed in Great Britain
by Amazon